Danay Donatien Martinez

Santerìa

The Definitive Guide to Cuban Santeria, Orishas, Yoruba History and the Rules for Becoming Iyawò

Table of Contents

Introduction

Congratulations on purchasing your copy of "Santerìa". It is a source of joy to me that you chose this book to delve deeper into the Yoruba religion.

In this book on Cuban Santeria, I wanted to delve into some aspects of the Yoruba religion that not everyone knows.

Therefore, after a brief introduction on the Afro origins of the Yoruba religion and the rules to respect in order to become a saint (Iyawò), I wanted to deepen some fewer known aspects through the stories of myths and legends.

In particular, I will explain who is Eshu ni Ipakò and its power, How the Shangò maraca was born, Ofun and the curious little girl and much more.

The goal of this book is to feed your curiosity of knowledge of Cuban Santeria.

Enjoy reading

Danay Donatien Martinez

Afro Origins: Cuban Santeria (Orishas)

The term "Santeria" was coined by the Spaniards to denigrate what seemed to them to be an excessive devotion to saints on the part of their slaves, who in this way failed to understand the main role of God in the Catholic religion. This attitude arose from a constraint imposed on them by the slavers: the strict prohibition, under penalty of death, to practice their animist religions brought with them from West Africa, forced them to find a solution to get around this prohibition and that is to hide, in the true sense of the word, behind Catholic iconography their Gods so as to be free to worship them without incurring the cruelty of the oppressor. In this way the Spanish rulers thought that the slaves, as good Christians, were praying to the saints when in fact they were actually preserving their traditional faiths. "Santeria" is, or has been, a derogatory term. Practitioners often prefer other names such as Lukumi or Regla de Ocha. However, the main deities of Cuban Santeria are similar if not identical to those of other African American religions. It is a kind of pantheon where, however, in addition to the various deities, there are abstract concepts demonstrating a fair level of religious, philosophical and metaphysical development. For example the trilogy Olofi-

Olordumare-Olorun that simplifying are the creator-the universal law-the vital force (a sort of Holy Trinity). They are the source of the Aché, the gift, the grace, the spiritual energy. For some people it is not a trilogy, but a single God, then Santeria would be a monotheistic religion, and the remaining Orishas of demigods (human beings who in life have done great things and once dead have been elected to the rank of gods) that personify nature with the function of messengers of the primordial divinity. The latter (about 400 in the original Yoruba religion, about forty in Santeria, of which only about fifteen are known to the majority of the faithful) remind us of Greek mythology with the various anthropomorphic deities at war, stealing each other's companions, taking revenge, raping, allying and protecting each other. The mythological tales of these divinities, not seldom in contradiction between them, are called Pattakìn .

Creation according to Yoruba beliefs

God Almighty, Holofi, lived in an infinite space, made only of fire, flames and dense steam. That was how Holofi wanted the universe. But the day came when he became bored with solitude and decided it was time to beautify that bleak and hostile landscape. He unleashed his power so that water came down in torrents. Some solid elements opposed his attack and so enormous chasms were formed in the rock: the vast and mysterious ocean where Olokun resides. In the most accessible points Yemaya took residence, vibrant in its colors, blue and silver. Yemaya was declared universal mother, mother of the Orishas. From her womb came the moon and the stars, the second step of creation. Olordumare, Obatalà, Olofi and Yemayà decided that the fire, extinguished in some areas, and still strong in others, would be completely absorbed by the bowels of the earth, through the feared and venerated Aggayù Sola, represented by the volcano and the mysteries of the depths. As the fire was extinguished, the ashes spread everywhere, forming the earth, represented by Orichaoko, which gave it strength enough to allow the birth of trees, fruits and herbs. In the woods wandered Osain, with his ancient wisdom on the medicinal powers of essences and herbs. Thus the swamps were also born. From those stagnant waters originated the epidemics, personified by Babalù Aye. Yemaya the wise, the generous, mother of all and of all, decided to give veins to the earth and created rivers of fresh and drinkable water, so that Olofi could create human beings. It was thus that Ochun was born. The two joined in an embrace of friendship that gave the world priceless wealth. Olofi decided to retire and live far away, behind the sun, Olorun, and left as his representative and executor of his orders Obatala, who created human beings. But a real disaster began. Obatala, so pure, white and clean, began to suffer from the intemperance of men. Tired of such filth, he rose up to live in the clouds. From there he began to observe the behavior of men and realized that something was wrong. Olofi had forgotten to create death.

Olokun is the mystery of the oceans. It is the most immense and profound thing imaginable, an entity so vast and mysterious that the human mind cannot conceive it and make a representation of it. Olokun is, together with Yemaya, the vital principle par excellence, the one from which everything springs. Precisely because of its immensity and its unthinkability, Olokun is the only Orisha of which it is not possible to make a material representation. No human being can be possessed by Olokun because its vastness could never be enclosed in such a limited body. It can be said that Olokun is a mystical entity to which believers turn with extreme awe and respect.

Orishas

The folkloric aspect of Santeria is closely linked to the ritual aspect. Music and dance play a fundamental role in practically all the rites of the Regla and derive directly from the African Yoruba tradition. The dances have as their main themes the rites of possession and trans and the representation of the lives and deeds of the various Orishas, each of which is symbolized according to a precise iconography. The tradition of ritual dance was then transferred outside the sacred rituals, codified and in a certain sense institutionalized until it became a folkloric artistic expression, but not for this reason emptied of its original meaning. The music that accompanies the rituals santeri is almost exclusively composed of rhythmic bases and vocal melodies in which alternates a dominant voice, called "Diana" or "cock", and a choir. The instruments used are drums and percussions called Batà, endowed with sacred value and jealously guarded together with the other sacred objects in the temple-houses, the Ilé Ochà, of the santeros and babalawos. Each Orisha and each ritual occasion corresponds to specific rhythmic sequences and combinations of instruments that accompany the course of the ceremony and play a central function in it of recalling the invoked spirits and offering to the Orishas. Ritual music can also be performed outside of ceremonies, as a folkloric artistic expression and, recently, several institutions have sprung up in Cuba with the aim of recovering and keeping alive the Yoruba musical tradition. Besides the many folkloric groups that operate in the country, two very famous interpreters of Yoruba songs (as well as famous santeros) are Lazaro Ros and Mercedita Valdés. The dance is also inspired by the rites of Yoruba origin. Each saint has its own characteristic movement that distinguishes it from the others. The Cuban regime considers these artistic expressions a cultural patrimony of the nation and has therefore elevated them to an academic level, revaluing their importance also for a political matter. Santeria in fact represents a valid instrument of opposition to Catholicism. Thanks to this have become famous in the world folkloric song and dance groups, such as the "Conjunto Folklorico Nacional", "Los Muñequitos de Matanzas", "Yoruba Andabo" and the composer Lazaro Ros.

Some of the main Orishas (saints) of Cuban Santeria

Elegguà

Orisha, protector of travellers, is the one who opens and closes roads and crossroads, who when he dances resembles a mischievous child. He holds the keys of destiny, he opens and closes the door to misfortune or happiness. It is the crossroads from which the roads of life branch out. He is Olofin's messenger and the first in everything. He has to be greeted before all the other Orishas, he is the first to receive the offerings (but also the last one, before saying goodbye), even the drums start for him and he has to be asked for his opinion before any divination, because he protects the paths of consultations and responses. He is catholicised with Saint Anthony of Padua, with the Spanish Nino de Atocha, but also with Anima Sola. His day is Monday, but many also celebrate him on the third day of each month. his colors are red and black. He is a major Orisha. He is the first of the group of four warriors (Eleggua, Oggùn, Ochosi and Osun). He instills a lot of fear because he has control over many things and often acts on a whim. He can be ruthless if you cross his path when he is angry. He is also prankster and playful; he can become irreverent as a brat, and is unpredictable, just like fate. It is the repository of Ashé, or spiritual power. He is also the symbol of opposites.

This Orisha, in the rites of divination, speaks and is represented through the numbers 3 and 21.

Oggun

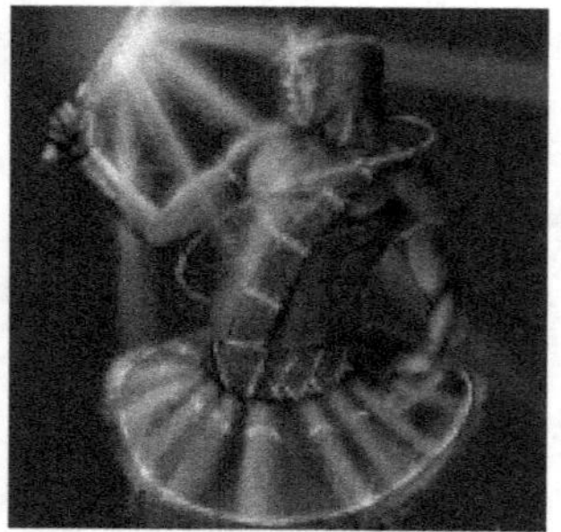

Oggùn is an Orisha feared for his unsociable nature and the power of his weapons. He is just the archetype of the violent manifestations inherent in human nature. His name means war, destruction, but also medicine, good and bad spirit. He is born from the bowels of the earth and his mission is to always war for all men, in religion and in life, since he committed the grave fault of abusing his mother Yemma when Yemayà taught him the art of love. Obatalà (his father) did not have time to curse him, because it was Oggun who condemned himself, hurling an anathema that would have prevented him from sleeping, during the day and the night, as long as the world would be world. He gets drunk with the guardian, to forget. According to an ancient Patakì (legend), he was seduced and then abandoned by the attractive Oshùn, who used his graces for the sole purpose of bringing him back to men, from whom he had detached himself out of disgust. He is in charge of providing nourishment to all the Orishas. He has many contacts with the Eggun, the spirits, and he likes witchcraft. Brother of Changò, violent and cunning, he is the god of minerals, mountains, and iron in general. Officially married to Oya, he has lost his wife who has become a faithful lover of Changò with whom he is in perpetual dispute. On earth he lives with Ochosi, at the side of the door of the house so that nothing bad can enter. He has numerous trails: from the strong and barbaric warrior to the sedentary peasant. Closer to human nature than to divine nature, this Orisha participates in all earthly anxieties and defects, and is a symbol of everyday life. He dominates keys, chains, the prison and metal in general, from machetes to cannons. In the shoulder he holds a tiger bag adorned with many shells. She dresses in green and around her waist she has a skirt made of palm fibres that protect her from the evils of life. Her necklace is made of alternating green and black balls. Her dance is very warlike, with a machete in her hand, but it also represents work, agricultural work or work with anvil and hammer. It protects against fever, surgery and, in general, against all damages caused by ferrous metals and accidents with blood loss. He is the protector of blacksmiths, mechanics, engineers, physicists and military. His days are Tuesday, Wednesday and the fourth of each month. He is syncretized with Saint Peter.

Changò or Shangò:

God of virility, masculinity, fire, lightning and thunder, war, Lord of the Bata drums, dance and music. Perhaps inspired by a mythical Yoruba king of the Oyo kingdom. Unwanted son of Yemayà, fruit of a rape, but protected by Obatalà. The Catholic saint is like Obatalà strangely feminine and is Saint Barbara. Her colors are white and red. and virile beauty. The word Changò means problem, in fact it represents all the virtues and all the human imperfections, he is worker, brave, good friend, soothsayer and healer, but he is also liar, womanizer, brawler and gambler.

His days are Fridays and the 4th of the month. Because of his wide concept of life and joy, it is said that he scares the dead. He certainly does not want to know suffering and pain. His objects are warlike: one and two strands axe, machete, spear, dagger, an arrow. He likes women and therefore has countless love affairs and quarrels with rivals. He has several mistresses, besides his official wives: Oyà, Obba Yurù and Ochun. When he begins to dance, he starts to give head blows, similar to those of the ram, towards the drums; he opens his eyes wide and shows his tongue; he waves his axe high and touches his testicles. Then begins the actual dance with jumps, contortions and extravagant figures. Her dance is warlike and erotic with accentuated movements of the pelvic fascia. As a deity of fire, she protects against burns and fires. She wears a necklace with alternating red and white beads. Red is a symbol of love and blood. She is always accompanied by Eleggua, of whom she is said to be Ocanani, which means made of one heart, inseparable. The nature of Changò finds its most evident representation in the fall of lightning, in the rapidity with which fire can devour everything it meets in its path. Legend has it that Ifà's divinatory abilities originally belonged to this Orisha, and that he gave them to Orula in exchange for skill in dance.

Ochùn or Oshùn

Goddess of love, beauty, femininity and rivers. The female counterpart of Changò (of whom she is the lover). Protected by Elegguà and Yemayà friend of Elegguà who protects her. Always accompanies Yemayà. She lives in the river and assists pregnant women and women in labor. She is represented as a beautiful mulatto, nice, a good dancer and always cheerful. She is capable of resolving, as well as provoking, quarrels between Orisha and men. Her color is yellow, but she is also attributed with teal and coral. It possesses healing virtues that it puts into practice through its waters and honey, of which it is the mistress. Her favorite flower is the sunflower. Her day is Saturday. Catholicised as the Virgin "de la Caridad del Cobre" (patron saint of Cuba). Ochun's colors (whose syncretic representation is the Virgin of Charity of Santiago) are yellow and gold, her number is 5. To her belong the royal peacocks other birds with colored plumage. Ochun is basically the representation of vanity and narcissism. She loves parties and dances, jewels and adornments of all kinds, especially gold.

Babalù Aye

Babalú Ayé: God healer of many venereal diseases, skin diseases, leprosy, cholera, infirmities in general etc.. For this reason it is associated to Saint Lazarus. The colors are white and blue. This in Africa was the main saint and most revered, in Havana there is a shrine in his honour (Rincon), where thousands of sick people go every year on December 17. He is one of the Orishas most invoked by the faithful in Santeria, but also by Cuban Catholics. It is the divinity that has to do with diseases of the body, epidemics, impairments. The representation of Babalu Aye, in fact, is that of a crippled beggar, covered with sores, dressed only in a very poor white robe. But Babalu Aye is also the one who helps those who suffer, the saint to whom everyone asks for the grace of healing and help in states of physical discomfort, health problems of their own or their loved ones. His messengers are flies and mosquitoes, because they carry diseases around. In the dance he arrives dragging himself like a sick person, wrapped on himself and, only in the final part - after having simulated a sort of rite of "limpieza" (cleaning)

Ochòsi

He is the third member of the group of Orishas called Guerreros and is delivered together with Eleggua, Oggun and Osun, the arrow of justice, to protect the one who receives this initiation, to open and pave his way. Ochosi is a hunter who, in pursuit of his prey, explores unknown and inaccessible territories. In the hierarchy of Orisha his role is that of intermediary and interpreter for Obatala, with whom he is in close relationship. Its colors are blue and yellow, its material representation is that of a rooster and its location within the house of the initiates is in an elevated place.

Obatalà

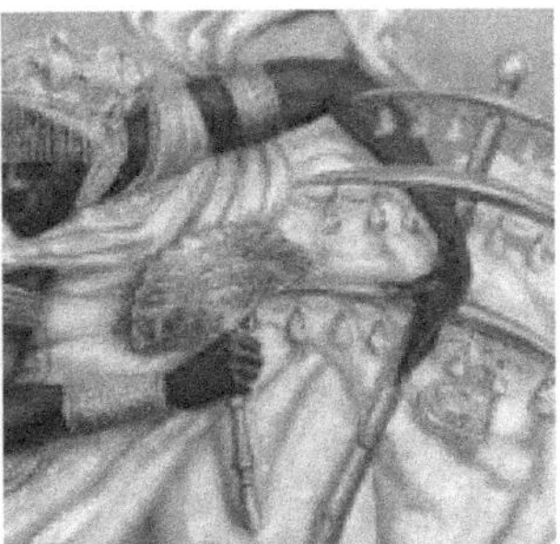

First among the Orishas. He is the saint dressed in white who protects, the mind, the head. Olofi created the universe, but gave Obatala the task of organizing the world and creating humanity. Pure deity par excellence, he loves peace and is merciful. He is the god of thought and dreams. He does not allow anyone to undress in his presence or to pronounce insulting or vulgar words. He is the only Orisha to have both male and female paths. According to his manifestation he can be male or female, old and wise or young and warrior. Catholicised as the Virgin "de la Mercedes".

Yemayà

Mother of life and of the other gods. Wife or, according to versions, daughter of Obatala. Goddess of salt water and therefore of the sea as a primordial source of life. Protector of women in labor, fishermen and sailors. Her anger is terrible, but always acts with justice. She loves good company; she is a good mother, cheerful and sanguine.

Her day is Saturday. When a woman is pregnant, she makes prayers so that the creature will be born well. In Yemayà love is born, not by chance she taught it to all Orisha. She was the wife of Babalù Ayé, of Agallù, of Orula and of Oggùn. Those who are consecrated to her cannot pronounce her name until they have touched the ground with the fingertips of their fingers and kissed the imprint of dust in them. There is a special bell to greet her and to attract her attention. She wears seven silver bracelets and seven skirts as if to represent the seven deep and mysterious seas. Her necklace is made of blue crystals and she wears a long robe of the same color with blue and white snakes. In the dance she announces herself with a thunderous laugh and then spins like the waves or eddies of the ocean. Sometimes he paddles, while others he seems to swim, but he always starts slowly to increase the intensity of the rhythm as with the threatening waves. Along with Changò and Ochun, it is among the Cubans' favorite. It corresponds to the Virgin Mary (Nuestra Señora de la Regla, patroness of the Bay of Havana).

Oyá

She is Changò's favorite woman, the mistress of the cemetery, she is also called Iyánsá meaning she is the mother who bore nine children. She is the mistress of the strong wind, such as hurricanes and whirlwinds. And the Orisha whose Catholic counterpart is the Virgen de la Candelaria (The Purification of the Virgin), that is Santa Teresita de Jesús, and the Virgen del Carmen.

Yewá

It is a superior Orisha. He lives in the cemetery among the graves and the dead is responsible for the corpses to deliver to Oya.

These are some of the major deities of Santeria. There are also a host of minor ones. The Yoruba belief system includes an omnipotent god (Olódùmarè) and 401 Irúnmöle. Of course there are no univocal rules on names, attributes and legends (patakìn of oral tradition catalogued only in the twentieth century). Rituals vary according to liturgical schools (reglas).

La Regla Conga or Palo Monte

This religious expression has its roots in religious cults of Bantu origin, a term used by Western ethnology to unite under a single name the community of peoples of Eastern, Central and Southern Africa who speak the same language in any of its variants. Also known as Mayombe, this rule was the result of the first transitions of Bantu faiths into Cuban society.

In the Conga rule, in general, is characteristic of connection with the forces of nature, of which some elements, such as vegetation, feel animated by spirits, where they take refuge as well as in the depths of the earth. The ancestors are represented in the water. The center of the ceremony in this belief is the Nganga, container in which there is supposed to be the soul of a dead person submitted to the will of the initiate through a pact that nourishes them both.

Danay Donatien Martinez

The Principle Of Good And Evil

The Manichaeism to which our rationalism has accustomed us does not exist here. "Every divinity contains within it the principle of good and evil."

To understand Cuban Santeria, one must return to West Africa. Immerse yourself in Yoruba culture. In the cult of the ancestors on which every village, even every family, based its religiosity. "These are the same divinities that, once they arrive on the American continent, lose all characteristics tied to the territory. Once likened to a river or a mountain, the Orishas become a generic representation of natural forces. They take on ideal anthropomorphic features, each symbolizing human qualities and flaws. The Yoruba pantheon includes a creator deity and numerous Orishas. "Each holds a particular power: strength, courage, reproduction." The Manichaeism to which our rationalism has accustomed us does not exist here. "Each deity contains within it the principle of good and evil." There is Oggùn, deity of iron and metals, who is soon assimilated with St. Peter. Babalù Aye, deity connected with the sick and disease, overlaps with St. Lazarus. Changò, deity of fire and lightning, of dance and war, becomes Saint Barbara. Eleggua is the symbol of opposites and protector of travellers. He is confused with St. Anthony of Padua.

"Orisha have human characteristics. That's why they are liked and revered to the extreme." Propitiatory practices exude passion. Veneration passes through moments of trance and altered states of consciousness. A fundamental ritual moment is that of possession, in which the evoked divinity enters the body of the faithful. It is one of the few moments in which the strong correspondence between natural elements - loss of consciousness, increased heartbeats, sweating - and properly cultural elements is evident. "It is the complete ecstasy to reach it is necessary to have a deep devotion". Also because the religions that come from Africa, unlike those of indigenous origin, do not foresee the use of drugs during rituals. Everything is justified by the faith of the believer. In compensation, there is often no lack of tobacco and rum. "But this is just another form of syncretism, the adaptation of these religious practices to the territory and society." A modernization. The same reason why Oggùn, deity of iron, over time has become the protector of railroad workers and policemen.

During the possession, the evoked deity enters the body of the believer. It is necessary to have a deep devotion. The rites do not involve the use of drugs, everything is justified by the faith of the believer.

In these religions there is no unanimously recognized hierarchical structure. The main priest of Santeria is the babalawo. "And with him are a series of helpers who allow the cult to take place," based on the similarities between the various African-derived cults. And then there are the initiates, who must first go through a rite of passage to become such. "After a ritual death, there follows a period of time in which one becomes 'nothing'. Tabula rasa. It is in this phase that one learns the complex rituals, the canticles, but also the way to fall into a trance and offer sacrifices to the deities." When one comes "back to life", even the physical appearance can be different. A rebirth that believers often show by shaving their hair. The celebrations take place in honour of the Orisha. They take place on the occasion of new initiations and according to the ritual calendar. And here are other syncretisms and correspondences with the Catholic world. Lemanja - divinity celebrated in Candomblé to which Yemayà corresponds in Santeria - protector of the sea and mother of all Orishas, overlaps with the Virgin Mary. It is not by chance that she is celebrated on December 8. Drums and dances are present in every ritual. Percussion has such a central role that it is even recognized as having a divine role. Without these instruments, after all, the divinities cannot be evoked during the celebrations. Divinities that manifest themselves through dance.

The animals to be offered to the Orisha in the sacrifices are carefully chosen. They are mainly chickening and kids, which are consumed by the believers during ritual berries.

Ritual sacrifices deserve a separate discussion. Orishas are paid homage with continuous offerings: almost always it is herbs and vegetables, elements that represent the strong link with nature. Yet sometimes the divinities feed on animal blood. "Blood is a fundamental element is relationship and communication". For this aspect, considered primitive and cruel, in some areas of South America these religions have long been persecuted. "Yet - insists the teacher - sacrifices in the past were also contemplated by the Catholic religion". The animals to be offered to the Orisha are carefully chosen. They are mainly chickening and kids, which are consumed by the believers during ritual berths. "In certain contexts, this is the only weekly opportunity for people participating in rituals to consume animal protein."

Unlike other cults with African roots, some say that Santeria involves only the use of white magic. This is an explanation dictated by anxiety about being recognized. According to some scholars, some rituals proper to Voodoo and Macumba have a merely symbolic meaning. "They are preparations that the priest advises the faithful to have an advantage in life. But since almost always, in order to achieve a goal, one must overcome someone's competition, these rituals serve to harm one's opponent." The preparations may contain clothes, hair or representations of the "enemy" But we can serenely consider these practices devoid of negative meanings. Also because these religions have as their sole purpose the pursuit of happiness. Unlike Catholic doctrine, there are no commandments to follow. Heaven is earthly. "The Christian religion refers to an extreme faith. It promises happiness in the Afterlife. These religions, on the other hand, struggle to achieve earthly happiness." But the goal cannot be achieved at all costs. "There are social rules that everyone must abide by. Everyone's fulfilment can never come through the unhappiness of others."

Danay Donatien Martinez

The "Three Circles" Of Yoruba

What is the Yoruba religion? The answer cannot be unambiguous. First of all, it is the religion of the Orisha, which arrived with the diaspora of slaves in Brazil and Cuba and spread massively after 1950, but it is also the Pentecostalism of many Nigerians who have emigrated in recent decades to European countries and those of Sub-Saharan Africa, especially to large cities like Nairobi and Johannesburg. Not only that, because at the same time there are Yoruba in Africa, some of whom, albeit with difficulty and compromise, continue to practice the "old religion", along with various forms of Islam and Christianity that those practices demonize. For the sake of clarity, let us distinguish "three concentric circles" of Yoruba religion, which are, from the innermost to the outermost:

1) the religion practiced by the Yoruba in their homeland, which is conventionally called "Yoruba traditional religion" (YTR) and which has at its core the worship of the orisha;

2) the religion followed by the vast majority of Yoruba today, consisting of various forms of Islam and Christianity (neo-Pentecostalism and other evangelical offshoots), oriented towards a general anti-Orisha sentiment;

3) the Yoruba religion that is practiced outside Nigeria in various parts of the world, by people who are not Yoruba or their descendants.

Between the first and third circles there is an intimate connection and at the same time a continuous contradiction. The cult of the orisha has had not only a lasting but also a growing impulse and flowering outside Africa, whereas at home these supernatural entities only dimly retain the importance they had in tribal cults before the dominant Christian and Muslim groups made them the object of theological attacks by declaring them "demonic.

Old and New Identity

At the base of the traditional Yoruba religion, in its two directions inside and outside Nigeria, is the YTR. First of all, because the term "Yoruba" itself, of Arab origin, was used to designate only the Oyo, one of the most important of the many ethnic groups that populated the region. Adopted by the Anglican missionary Church in 1840, the name was extended to all the local populations that it was intended to evangelize, similar in language and culture and, above all, who considered themselves descendants of Ife-Ife.

These diverse groups found greater unity, however, in the context of slavery in the Americas, where they also often had to defend themselves against other very different African ethnic groups such as the Lucumi in Cuba, the Nago in Brazil and the Aku in Sierra Leone. What, more than all the different origins or affiliations, counts in the "Yoruba" identification is the devotion to the orisha, which can manifest itself in Nigeria in an extreme variety of local forms different from city to city; for example Shangò, who plays a predominant role in the South American cult, was an oyo deity practically ignored by the eastern ethnic groups; Oduduwa was an ancestral (male) commander of Ife in the central-eastern regions while she is considered the (female) consort of the god of creation in the southwest; among river deities, Yemoja belonged mainly to the west, Osun to the center and east while Oya, connected to the Niger River and tornadoes, to the north. Geographical location favoured the western regions, home to the preeminent Oyo and from which Islam had arrived, over the more remote east and its inaccessible forests.

New World

The flow of Yoruba slaves to the Americas was continuous and massive especially between the 1810s and 1826-50, a period when the social and political weakening of the Oyo left a power vacuum and decades of internecine wars, until well after the abolition of slavery by France and Britain in the 1930s as human trafficking continued through illegal routes to the Spanish and Portuguese colonies, where slavery was later abolished (in Cuba in 1886, in Brazil in 1888). The ability of these cults to survive adversity and change while maintaining a strong African connotation is, therefore, due to their adaptability, but also to a series of other circumstances: for example, in the colonies of Latin America, Catholic missionaries and evangelizers were better prepared than their Protestant and Anglican counterparts to recognize and accept the existence of different African nations and allow them to associate in a limited sphere of activity, a condition that understandably favoured the survival of the traditions; the cabildos, missionary institutions, had this aggregative function and, at the same time, provided an important framework within which to maintain the cult of the orisha in a process of syncretic dissimulation with Catholic saints and their Iberian-Baroque iconography.

Necessity of adaptation and new inspirations have therefore led to a reduction in the number of deities, present in indefinite quantity in the traditional religion; the main "survivors" (Sango, Ogun, Yemoja, Esu-Elegba, Obatala, Ososi, Osun, Oya, Sopona or Babaluaye) have in common that they come from the central and north-western regions of Yorubaland, in particular Sango who is a royal god for the Oyo and who also in America has assumed a prominent position to the point of eclipsing even, in some cases, the importance of the others (think of the Brazilian Xango or the Shango of Trinidad). Other orisha have disappeared in certain regions and flourished in others - Orunmila, for example, is almost non-existent in Brazil while in Cuba it is the object of great devotion.

The complex rituals of Yoruba derivation then developed a modern, rational theological and ritual organization in response to the impact with a non-African context and using its tools as a resource. This transformation of the religion of the Orisha into a true belief system involved a sort of "pantheonization" of the cult under the banner of unification and hierarchy, similar to what is found in Greco-Roman religion; but it is a deceptive road to travel, an abstraction, when the concrete reality consists instead of many different cults in a variety of forms that change, in the land of origin, from region to region. Here, unlike in the New World colonies, the Orisha have never shared festivals or temples, and indeed their relations are marked by open rivalry with each other.

Hence the religion of the orisha in the Americas seems to take two different paths, the first marked by African Americans and the other, in particular, by the santeros of Cuba, where in the late nineteenth century five Yoruba babalawo established the Regla de Ifa and founded its main branches.

Re-Africanization and universalism

The "third circle" (the expansion of the religion of the Orisha outside Africa) includes two different lines of historical development: that of the contraction, in Nigeria, of the cult of the Orisha and the opposite and contrary line of expansion in the radically new context of the diaspora. These two directions produced, on the one hand, the desire of Yoruba African Americans for a "return to Africa", a revisionism that would provide answers to the need for ethnic integrity, and, on the other, the Yorubización, an inclusive opening supported above all by the Cubans, who had introduced the religion of the Orisha into the United States at the end of the 1940s. Afro-Cuban religions are in fact characterized by a "theology of non-racially marked recruitment" because in Cuba these cults did not identify with blackness, as on the contrary happened in the United States.

The most concrete result of the first current was the founding of a village in South Carolina, called Oyotunji (Oyo Revived), still active and operating today. In this place, a Yoruba community has literally reinvented itself, respecting a cycle of ceremonies dedicated to the major orisha and appealing to divination to learn about its African ancestors. Its founder, the Oba Adefunmi (Walter S. King by birth), first lived through a more eclectic phase, today one would say "open to contamination" (especially from the Aka and Dahomei) until, towards the end of the 1950s, he formed a special bond with a Santero, Cristóbal Oliana, and then turned sharply towards the political positions of black nationalism. The result on the religious level was, on the one hand, the refusal to accept that non-black people could be initiated into the traditional religion, and on the other hand, the need for legitimacy coming directly from the Oni of Ife, the highest authority on the matter. According to this orientation, in fact, the "primordial" ritual and doctrinal formulas, coming from Ife-Ife as the place of cosmogony, have a greater effectiveness. But African Americans on this side of the Atlantic did not suspect that, paradoxically, this charge is, if not a Christian subject, at least strongly influenced by the Pentecostal presence of the dominant community; and that for their part, Nigerians consider the "new" Yoruba of Adefunmi as oyimbo ("Europeans," no more than outsiders).

In Nigeria, Islam and Christianity are the foreign and hegemonic religions with respect to the indigenous population, which suffers their influences: the Church of Orunmila, for example, founded in the 1920s, models its services on those of the Protestant churches, with a result that is anything but primitive and original.

But on the fortunate wings of this need for recognition flew many episcopal advantages, ceremonial experts and babalawo, the best known of whom was Professor Wande Abimbola, Ifa's spokesman in the world on behalf of the Ooni himself, whose task is to promote Nigerian Yoruba practice as "normative" and who has found greater support in Brazil than in Cuba, where the Regla de Ifa prevails.

To the profound decline of traditional religion in Yorubaland corresponds, in America, the search for an original wisdom to which to refer and by which to feel legitimized, becoming the means for a tradition that one would like to be uninterrupted. Spurious elements are expunged in respect of a re-Africanization that becomes a sort of "desyncretization", in sharp contrast with the accommodating and dogma-free nature of the religion of the orisha, that ability to mix-and-match with the variegated forms of African Protestantism, with the even more aerial new age spirituality or with other non-Yoruba African traditions capable of creating syncretic products continually distinguished by the freshness of contemporaneity.

It must be admitted that the Yoruba are no longer the primary vectors of their own traditional religion, but Afro-Caribbeans and African-Americans are no less so now than devout Latinos. Santeria and Candomblé are the classic examples of a good result in adapting flexibly to the point of losing any obligation with the ethnolinguistic provenance, the first requirement for that of the Orisha to aspire to become a World religion of the third millennium.

Danay Donatien Martinez

How To Be Crowned A Saint

Making yourself the Saint or crowning Osha is like emerging from the water

Let's start by reviewing what is referred to when it is said that someone will be Crowned a Saint. The saint crowning ceremony is called Kari Osha or Ijoko Osha and it transforms the neophyte (Aleyo) into a Santero or Santera (Olorisha). The ceremony of crowning a Saint (Osha) is quite long and laborious, in this ceremony the guardian angel of the aleyo crowns his head, and it is called the crowning of the Saint. From that moment, the person becomes one with his guardian angel (Osha tutelary), this is one of the most important and transcendental decisions that any human being can make and that is why it is advisable to know what is necessary and relevant before giving this big step.

Anciently it was recommended that the future Olorisha, arrived in the room of the Holy with the least possible knowledge of religion, but this has caused hundreds, perhaps thousands of people cheated throughout the American continent ending up in disappointment and misunderstanding of the priesthood. To avoid this I leave you with, some things you should and can know:

A plate, two coconuts and two candles: the first sacrifice

The person in need of Ijoko Osha, i.e. the neophyte or uninitiated practitioner, must come to the home of the godfather or godmother of his choice with the offering of a plate, two coconuts, two candles and a certain amount of money that varies according to the Ilè Osha, and place them in front of the guardian angel of the godfather or godmother and agree with him on the moment when he will "give coconut" to the guardian angel of the godfather or godmother to know if the guardian angel of the latter will accept him as a son and give birth to his Osha*.

At the time of "giving coconut" to the Guardian Angel of the godfather or godmother, the Ijoko Osha applicant must be present in addition to several witnesses attesting to the ceremony.

The godfather or godmother may refuse to perform this ceremony for any reason, without having to give any explanation or simply explain what is appropriate.

The godparent or godmother, upon agreement with the uninitiated practitioner, also "gives coco" to his or her Guardian Angel to determine who will be the Oyugbona. Once it has been determined who the Oyugbona will be, one goes to his or her home, is informed of the situation to get his or her approval and, if he or she agrees, the Oyugbona's Guardian Angel should also be "given coco" so that his or her approval or otherwise is known.

The godfather or godmother surely knows that any incompetence, neglect, shameful, disrespectful acts, crimes and misdemeanours, and acts against the individual and society of their godchildren constitute a disgrace to the godfather or godmother. All bad deeds, in one way or another, go against the prestige and authority of the godfather or godmother and fall on their religious family. So something as sacred as Osha should not be given to them without first being very careful and cautious.

The godfather or godmother should be careful when the Ijoko Osha applicant is an uninitiated practitioner belonging to another Ilè Osha and should investigate well the usual strict arguments.

The neophyte and uninitiated practitioner should provide sufficient evidence to the godfather or godmother that he will be able to abide by the rules of Osha, Ifà and his Ità and until he shows evidence of this, the godfather or godmother should not initiate him.

The prospective godfather or godmother should provide documentation of the rules or regulations of Osha and Ifà so that the prospective initiate knows what he or she is facing and what he or she must abide by.

The godfather or godmother should answer as many questions as possible and clarify any doubts about what Ifà is and its obligation to comply.

The godfather or godmother will introduce the neophyte to his future religious brothers and sisters and in general to his future religious family so that they may begin to strengthen the necessary bonds of brotherhood and increase the sense of belonging to their religious branch.

The future "Iyawó" will have to study all the documentation provided to him by his godfather or godmother and will ask the necessary questions to clarify parts that he does not understand well.

The future initiate will be informed if there are any members in his biological family, deceased or not, who are or were related to Osha and Ifà and to which branch they belong or belonged and what levels of consecrations they have or had. This information will be provided to your sponsor when requested.

* In my case, Oshun rejected several godchildren. He did not want to welcome them as sons. Each head chooses its own home, but we can't know that until Osha lets us know for sure. Oshun safeguards, protects, welcomes, but doesn't always decide to bear children for everyone and take responsibility for following everyone. So if Oshun doesn't accept you, don't take it wrong, surely your head wants to be born to another Osha.

Iyawó: First Year Of Priesthood Rules

Who is Iyawó?

He is a newly initiated priest. The word Iyawó means "bride of mystery". The priest is considered Iyawó for the first year and seven days after his initiation. But in some religious this period of energetic assimilation of her Orisha Alagbatori is determined differently.

Striking by the whiteness of his clothes, he is purifying all evil from his life before his coronation or "Kariosha". He has "made himself holy" to protect himself from some future illness or misfortune. Iyawó do not shake hands and should not frequent public places or cemeteries. Nor can they be away from home when the sun sets, much less when the sun is in the middle of the sky at noon. During those times, they should have a roof over their heads.

The Iyawó is a believer who has just been "born again" because he is born to religious life and dies to secular life. He must wear white for one year and seven days. White clothing indicates a spiritual readiness to connect with the divine. Their head is covered by a cap or turban and their shirts are long-sleeved for the first three months. He cannot bathe in rainwater nor stand in the wind of thunderstorms.

His consecration takes place over a period of seven days, where he remains in the "Igbodu" on a throne alluding to his Orisha Tutelare. During those first days, the Iyawó in silence, rests, meditates and is in recollection. He cannot speak; children do not speak. If he does, he must measure his words very well: they could be prophetic sentences.

Friday is the day to give acquaintance to Oshun on the river, Saturday is the consecration ceremony, Sunday is a festival where the Iyawó wears his coronation costume and receives visitors from 2:00 to 6:00 p.m., as well as sharing a large meal for lunch. Monday is the day of Itan Imale of the Orisha who were born with him: they give him advice for the future. The following Tuesday and Wednesday, the Iyawó is on retreat. On Thursday morning, the Iyawó will go to the square to feed Eshu who lives in the market and pay homage to the deity Oyà. Then he will go to the Church to ask for the Blessing of Olofi, represented in the Blessed Sacrament, and light a white candle in his honour.

In order to understand the Yoruba ethic, it is necessary to know how the myth tells the process of destiny at the moment the individual comes to Earth. For the Yoruba, according to Oddú Babá Irosun Melli, "there is no one who comes into the world without their time." When the energy of an Oddun descends to Earth for an initiate, the warnings-which are not always prohibitive-are the conditions the person has chosen in heaven for his or her life project on this plane, his or her destiny.

The ìyáboraje or ìyáboraggio, or period in which the practitioner of our Religion is of Iyawó, lasts twelve months and a few days that depend on the Orisha to which his head has been consecrated or the lineage or House of the Saint to which he belongs. This period is regulated by a set of rules that, in the case of the Afro Cuban Osha Rule, were established in the Council of 1904, held in the city of Regla, Cuba, when the elders of this religion decided to unify the doctrine.

It is not uncommon to see an Iyawó dressed all in white with the idé of the Orisha who "crowned himself" and his necklaces, but with modern clothes and an unscrupulous walk. But there is free will, any disrespect to the rules of the Iyawó are a disrespect to the Crown one wears on his head. Where there is no respect, there is no sacredness.

Clothing

Must dress in white for one year both on the street and in the home and sleep dressed in consecration clothing (socks, hat, briefs or underwear and pajamas).

To leave the house he must be properly dressed. Clothing must be clean and not torn.

The Iyawó man must go out in the street dressed with closed shoes, socks, underpants, shirt, pants, handkerchief and long-sleeved shirt; on your head he must wear the cap of the Igbodun under the hair and use an umbrella. What changes after the first three months is that he can go out in a short-sleeved shirt or blouse. All clothing must be completely white, except for times when he must be dressed another way due to his profession or job. Inside he will have a white fabric to protect his body. In this case it is asked in Itá.

The Iyawó woman must go out in the street dressed in closed shoes, long socks, underwear, skirt, scarf and a blouse with sleeves. On her head she must have a handkerchief and a turban and use an umbrella. After the first three months she may go out wearing only the veil and the rest of her clothing must be completely white, except at times when for reasons of profession or trade she must dress otherwise. Inside she will have a white fabric to protect her body. In this case it is asked in Itá.

Male Iyawó may not wear shorts or tight-fitting dresses; Women may not wear low-cut blouses, suspenders or body-hugging skirts, shorts or leggings of any kind. No Iyawó should wear see-through clothing.

Iyawó shall walk out with all sacred necklaces, handles and Iddé that were placed during Yoko Osha. They should not wear body adornments such as rings, chains, bracelets and other items not related to the worship of Osha and Ifá.

They should not paint or remove their eyebrows, paint their lips or nails, their hair cannot be dyed. Nor may they be trimmed during the first three months as Iyawó, nor may they undergo perms or beauty treatments.

She should not look in the mirror or comb her hair during the first three months and should not use perfume or cosmetics during the Iyawó year.

She should bathe with unscented or very faintly smelling soaps. Excluded from this rule are all those who by profession or trade are obliged to do so or who due to the characteristics of their metabolism must use some kind of deodorant, lotion or cream to avoid strong body odour or any particular condition of the body.

To go out you must always wear closed shoes, that is, you cannot wear open shoes such as flip flops, sandals, etc.. This rule applies to both men and women.

Iyawó and Olosha should know that never again in their life they should wear black, except in the case of the performance of a certain ceremony (only the Olosha) or for reasons related to their profession or trade about which it is necessary to ask in Itan of Yoko Osha.

Like to sleep

The Iyawó man must sleep in socks, underwear, shirt, hat and pajamas.

The woman must wear short socks, underwear, bodice, hat or handkerchief and robe.

For the remainder of his or her life, the priest will not be able to sleep in the nude or shirtless.

His sheets and towels must be white and clean, just like the rest of his clothes.

In order to sleep, he must remove his religious attributes (necklaces and handles), except for the Iddé de Orula and the white metal handle of Obatalà, since they are a protection even during sleep.

The initiate, male or female, at the foot of the bed must have a pair of flip-flops, because the Iyawó does not put his bare feet on the floor.

With sleeping clothes he does not stand on the doorstep or leave it.

He sleeps with a dim light in the room and at home there must always be a light on or dimmed at night.

Visiting Ilé Osha

The Iyawó, to visit religious houses for the first time, must be accompanied by his Oyugbona, godfather or godmother or one of the witnesses of his Osha. After that you may visit that Ilé on your own.

Oyugbona is obligated to take the Iyawó to the Ilé Osha of the witnesses of his consecration ceremony and Itá, where they can give him a plate, two candles, two coconuts and ten pesos and other items of his choice.

The godfather or godmother is the one who brings the Iyawó to visit his godfather from Awofakán ni Orunmila or Ikofafún ni Orunmila so that he can talk to him through the Itá Osha Notebook (Itan Imalè) and that conversation is noted therein.

Food and Nutrition of Iyawó

Iyawó must eat on a mat for three months. Throughout the year he must eat with the spoon, plate and glass that have been consecrated to Igbodun and cannot eat with a knife and fork. He must go out with the glass, plate and spoon in case he has to eat food on the street. The Iyawó should not eat standing in the street.

In case he is in another Ilé Osha or in someone's house, he must do so sitting on a mat as the rule states.

The leftovers of what he eats are dedicated to Eshu or Egun and are collected with a piece of paper and placed in the street in front of the door of the house.

Iyawó who eat at work or for other reasons of their profession and trade are excluded from these rules; not so at home or in some Ilé Osha.

Iyawó must keep the spoon, plate and glass of consecration because if they become ill, these are the utensils to be used to obtain a speedy recovery.

Exit home

The Iyawó, during the first three months, may not leave the house before 6 a.m. and must be in the house before 6 p.m. at night. After the first three months, he must be in his own home before midnight.

All those who by profession or trade need to break the rules, are obliged to ask for it in the Ità of Yoko Osha. In case of emergency he will do it covered with a white cloth or a white sheet. In case of exception, he will cover his head with both hands.

At 12 o'clock in the day and 12 o'clock at night he must be indoors. He should not travel on roads or dark places, nor walk in the sun. All those who by profession or trade need to do so, are obliged to ask for it in the Itá of Yoko Osha. In case of emergency it is covered with a white cloth or sheet. Finally, the head is covered with both hands.

When the sun's rays fall perpendicular to the Iyawò's position on the earth, he/she should keep his/her head covered, at least, with a white cloth.

The Iyawó should remain at home most of the time and go out only for necessary obligations. He/she should go outside with a white umbrella and walk through the shady part. He should avoid direct sunlight, but should sunbathe at appropriate times -

morning from 8 a.m. to 10 a.m. and afternoon from 4 p.m. to 5 p.m. Iyawó should avoid the sun's rays at noon.

Iyawó should not go out on the street when natural disasters or severe weather events are announced or occur, and should not stand on doors or windows during that inclement weather. In the event of an emergency, protect your head and follow the instructions of the appropriate authorities.

The Iyawó never goes out alone.

He should not sit in parks, should not stand on street corners, should not go to bars, night clubs, cabarets, market square, prisons, ruins, cemeteries, funeral homes, funerals or hospitals, much less to see the seriously ill. Excluded are those who have close relatives who are seriously ill as long as visits are made with prudence and with the permission of the godfather or godmother, having made the appropriate arrangements. Also excluded are those who are obliged to do so because of their profession or trade. In any case, the Obbá should ask for it on the Itá day of Yoko Osha.

Social and public activities of Iyawó

The Iyawó should not go to public parties, dances, carnivals or costume parties, nor should he participate in assemblies. All those who by profession or trade need to do so are obliged to ask for it in the Yoko Osha.

The Iyawó should not travel by air or sea without the permission of his guardian angel.

He should not be in dark places such as cinemas or other places, and not in houses in the same condition. All those who by profession or trade need to do so, are obliged to ask for it in the Itá of Yoko Osha.

Sexual Life

The Iyawó must try not to have sexual relations to the best of his or her ability until sixteen days after the conclusion of his or her consecration and must abstain from promiscuous relations throughout his or her life.

Godchildren of the same godfather or godmother and Oyugbona may not choose within the same religious family with whom to have sexual relations, as they are siblings.

Religious greeting

In public spaces, Iyawó should greet all elders (Olosha, Babalosha, Iyalosha, Babalawo, and Oluwo) and also other Iyawó who take the initiative, asking for a blessing and crossing their arms over their chest. In religious spaces, it must be done in the established manner.

When he meets his godfather or godmother or his Oyugbona, in religious places, he should throw himself on the ground as a sign of respect for the Guardian Angel of his elders.

All Olosha, Babalosha, Iyalosha, Babalawo or Oluwo have a duty to lift from the ground the minor who is greeting them. The Iyawó greets the elders one by one.

Other rules, even for Olosha

- The Iyawó or Olosha must know that he cannot touch his Osha and Orisha during menstruation, nor participate in initiations, consecrations, ceremonies, rituals or consultations.
- During the first three months, the Osha's and Orisha's of the Iyawó will remain on a mat on the floor receiving irradiation from the Iyawò's house. Thereafter they are

consulted with "the coconut" and will get up from the floor and stand in a certain position according to the Iyawò's Guardian Angel.

- She should bathe in the house twice a day, when she gets up and before she goes to sleep, in both cases with lukewarm water.

- His godfather or godmother, Oyugbona or elder brother, has the power to require him to abide by his Ità, Osha Ifà rules and religious commitments to his elders. But no one can stop him from leading a normal life that has nothing to do with religion. This is your choice. Oloddumare will judge in the end.

- He will need to put a little cocoa butter on his head every day.

- He may not throw the Diloggun or participate in rites and ceremonies, much less actions against anyone, or enter the home of any Olosha or Babalawo when rites and ceremonies are performed, or go to spirit centres.

- The Iyawó must receive the Room of the Saint (Igbodun) after realizing Ebbó Oshumeta and completing the year of Yoko Osha.

- He may never enter an Igbodun until he has made Ebbo Oshumeta and has duly received Igbodun. He should know that any religious curiosity should be cleared with his godfather.

- The Iyawó or Olosha should know that of the Ebbó animals, the Obbà is the first to be chosen, the second is the Oyugbona and the third is the Afeisitá.

- He will be obliged to communicate with his elders when something harmful to his life happens.

- He must not violate the Rules for Santeros. The Iyawó is a sacred status. During the year and the days in which one is Iyawó, the person begins to purify some of the negative aspects of the previous life and during that phase one may experience very difficult situations, which intensify and become more serious with non-compliance.

- In the event that the Iyawó cannot do the Ebbò within his home, he must give "entry" to his Osha in his own home by feeding Eleguá.

- The Iyawó, Olosha, Babalosha and Iyalosha should not pass over holes or sewers and be very careful when entering caves, tunnels, garbage dumps, forests or mountains; they should not cross pipes. However, in this regard one should always ask in Itá de Yoko Osha whether for reasons of his work or trade the Iyawó should be in those circumstances.

- Iyawó shall not be allowed to bathe in the sea, beach, river, swimming pool, well, lagoon, dam or pool of water. Except for those who by profession or trade must do so. (Divers, rowers, lifeguards). In this specific case you must ask in Itá.

- He may not give parties or dances in the house where he has his Osha for the duration of the Iyawó year.

- He must not give or receive anything from anyone's hands. What will be offered to an Iyawó or given to him is done on the carpet or floor.

- He may not ask anyone for fire to light cigarettes, nor give it, and should avoid smoking during that year, much less may he smoke from a cigarette lit by another person.

- The Iyawó should not dance or spin, should not run and less behind any object or vehicle, should not climb stairs leaning against the wall, or scaffold, or on roofs or trees; should not walk on walls, should not jump on the spot or jump from one place to another and should not get wet with rainwater. Excluded are those who, because of their profession or trade, must do so: dancers, builders, etc. In this case it is asked in Itá.

- Iyawó must take care to ride motorcycles, tricycles, bicycles, strollers, skates, skis, vehicles towed by others and, if he must drive, he must do so with great caution and care. When driving he may look in the mirror because he is not looking at himself. Iyawó may not be hung from the door of any vehicle.

- Iyawó should not wait in line, walk behind people or go through groups of people who are parked. If the Iyawó is required to "stand in line," he should approach his godfather, siblings and religious elders or biological family so that they can stand in line for him. He should always avoid riots and gatherings of people.

- Iyawó may not be portrayed, filmed or made on television, except for his profession, trade or some special reason. In this regard, he is obligated to ask in Itá about Yoko Osha.

- Iyawó cannot allow himself to be performed any ritual by anyone other than his godfather or godmother.

- You may relate to other branches of Osha Ifá or other religions, but you must not betray your Osha or your family.

- Iyawó and Olosha have religious domicile in the home of his godfather or godmother where they should always be welcomed and protected under all circumstances. However, they must not compromise the freedom or legality of your religious family.

- The Iyawó shall not kill another person except in self-defence or in defense of his country against an aggressor.

- The figure of the Iyawó must be carefully respected, they are the living representation of Osha. Iyawó must be aware of the respect they owe to their status.

- In the worship of Osha and Ifà there is respect for seniority and elders. There is a special attitude towards the mentally retarded, the disabled, and caring people towards drunks and crazy (mentally unbalanced) people.

- The Iyawó should not curse himself or any other person, should not swear or wish for death. And he should keep murky thoughts out of his mind.

- The Olosha should not commit suicide or murder or homicide. Only Oloddumare determines his journey to Ará Onú. However, the Olosha is obligated to defend his life, his Osha, his family, his home, and the land of his birth, even if he must expose his own life or break the lives of others.

- He will avoid arguments and verbal or physical insults to other people, especially with his family, spouse and religious relatives. Iyawó should not hit children or punish them and should heed what they say and pay attention to them.

- You should not drink alcoholic beverages or use any kind of drugs.

- Iyawó and Olosha should avoid having sex and being naked in the same room as his Osha and Orisha. If he doesn't have another room, he should take the necessary steps to do what he wants in privacy by putting up a curtain, protection, sheet, etc.

- Iyawó should not walk around the house naked, much less look at himself naked in mirrors.

- The priest should not be related to theft, fraud, embezzlement, crime, drug trafficking and selling, or activities involving the abuse of weak persons or affecting the community or individuals.

- Iyawó and Olosha may not carry sharp weapons or blunt objects for aggressive purposes, carry or possess firearms for any purpose. Except those who by profession or trade must possess them. In this case you ask in Itá.

- The Iyawó should not make inappropriate comments or repeat undesirable things or promote gossip, make improper inquiries, much less talk about uncertain things. He should not use obscene words or make inappropriate gestures, or express yourself brazenly so that your religious and moral status is not affected.

The Riches That Olokun Gives In Eyirosun

The Cuban Santeria is full of legends that are told whenever an oracular sign of the Diloggun appears on the mat. Each one of them encloses not one, but several messages that the consultant will be able to realize in his existence. Like this message of promised wealth that is achieved simply by giving your best in your employment, despite your employer not recognizing your worth. In the end, it is cunning that pays off.

Where is this legend found? In the corpus of Eyirosun, four mouths of the shells that reveal the will of the Orisha. Also known as Iroso or Irosun. Sign loved by Olokun, the deity of the ocean depths.

The young apprentice who adored Olokun

Once a Babalawo who tanned hides had an apprentice to whom he paid a nickel and offered him lunch and dinner.

Every morning that boy would go to the seashore, greet Olokun and ask for gold and good luck.

Another Babalawo who had seen him making his prayers in the sea told his master and the latter followed him to see if it was true. He caught him, paid him and then fired him.

Four months after this happened, the boy apprentice met a man who was looking for a young labourer. The man gave him the job on the condition that he enter the house blindfolded. He agreed and the man took him to a house full of gold and gave him a small key to open three different doors blindfolded. While he was inside, he ordered him to clean the gold that was there, and when he was finished he paid him twenty-four gold coins and then dismissed him. Soon this man died. He had no one to inherit his property, and the rulers of that country put the house up for sale. The boy showed up and offered more than the others if they would let him see it first. He knew the secret of the doors, and with a false key he opened them and found bars of gold, a sack of pearls and another of diamonds. To the others, who did not know the secret, it seemed absurd to offer what the house was not worth, and the boy became immensely rich.

So he went to find the Babalawo who had been his teacher and gave him the five cents he had earned at his side. He continued to greet Olokun every day at the seashore for making him rich.

This is the reason why the Iyawó enters the Igbodu blindfolded and Eyiorosun Meyi's ebb must be made by the Babalawo with different skins, twenty-four coins as compensation, a casserole of fine corn, four ekó, blue handkerchief, seven coconuts, green banana and flags, three roosters, a coral necklace, two doves and two parrot feathers.

Who is Olokun?

Olokun is the personification of several human characteristics, such as patience, meditation, observation, and future visions. His characteristics are found and visible on the ocean floor. Olokun governs material wealth, psychic abilities, dreams, meditation, and mental health.

In Afro-Cuban cults, Olokun is connected to Yemaya, as both are associated with the same element of nature, the sea, water.

In its female version, Olokun is the wife of Olorun and the mother of Obatala..

The Sixth Sense Of Eshu Ni Ipakò

Eshu ni Ipakò is a deity that few people are familiar with. They have heard of it but do not know much about it. Eshu ni Ipakò is nothing but the most important manifestation of Eshu in the lives of human beings. It represents the spirituality that inhabits the human cerebellum. It is the interface that processes the information of the brain and connects it with the motor instincts of the body and vice versa.

How do the energies affect Eshu ni Ipakò?

Eshu ni Ipakò acts like a radio transmitter in the sense that it captures every influence, no matter how slight, and transmits it to Opolo and by extension to Ori Inu. Ori Inu is perfect and is our connection to Olofin, but Opolo is not since it is formed from matter and only works on the earth here.

When we think of our inner self we hear a voice that goes to direct our thoughts: this is our Ori Inu. Orì Inu is influenced by the intervention of other areas of the body, but without the intervention of Eshu or Ipakò it would simply be impossible for such intervention to occur.

Eshu ni Ipakò is not only physical, it has a direct connection with Orun (Onù), it is as if an energy flows from the head, arms and legs that gathers there, and in fact that is what happens. Eshu ni Ipakò receives what comes from the outside and emanates what comes from the inside.

So our first exercise is to focus our breath on our Eshu ni Ipakò, which we will do in the morning and at night before we go to sleep; this will help our Eshu ni Ipakò to have more channels open.

How does energy transmission occur?

Eshu ni Ipakò uses the central nervous system. When someone approaches you and you feel cold or skin cramps, you are sensing that an Arà Orun phenomenon was coming with that person and your Eshu ni Ipakò detected it. Subsequently, Eshu ni Ipakò manipulated your central nervous system to let you know. You can use any of the 5 senses: taste, touch, sight, smell, and hearing. In which of these senses would you place cold? You might say in touch, but there is a gap because to be stimulated touch must touch something. Well, cold tells us that there is a sixth sense that is imposing and overwhelming because no matter what we are doing, it just steps in! That sixth sense is Eshu ni Ipakò.

The influence of Eshu ni Ipakò on the central nervous system

Eshu ni Ipakò is located in the cerebellum. Since we know from the study of medicine that external stimuli are conducted to the brain through neurons in the spinal cord, this stimulus is filtered in the cerebellum and guided to the specific part of the brain where it is processed and then relayed back to the area that emitted it and generates a response.

In the case of Eshu ni Ipakò as the immediate recipient of the stimulus, it emits the signal to the sense receptor so that it captures the stimulus and sends it to the brain following the regular process of the central nervous system. It is as if the stimulus came from within the being, as if an alarm was triggered and directed the senses to the exact point of its origin. In this sense, the person thanks to Eshu ni Ipakò can become aware of supernatural phenomena occurring around him - but this faculty must be educated and developed. The principle of this development is to concentrate by breathing into our Eshu ni Ipakò and meditating on this phenomenon.

When we perform the mojugba of summoning to the ancestors, the Orisha or spirits, manifest in our Eshu ni Ipakò and it is then that the divinatory phenomenon occurs.

How can we propitiate Eshu ni Ipakò?

We can start with breathing exercises and meditation; they give him reinforcement.

Then we can move on to different Ebbomisi to refresh him with the herbs (ewe) of our main Oddun. So-called Oddun contains the main recommendations of Ifa and Orisha and clarifies the herbs (ewe) that favor us.

We can also offer sacrifice to Ojiji (the shadow), which is directly related to Eshu ni Ipakò.

But above all improving it will be the consequence of our activities and of course religious practice.

Curiosity about Eshu ni Ipakò

This Eleggua lives at the base of the neck behind the cerebellum (Ipakò) and connects us to the world of Orun, which is why it is said to be related to the sixth sense.

It is of utmost importance because it represents our very existence in the world manifesting as our astral shadow.

This Orisha is not to be received in religious ceremonies, it accompanies us from our birth.

When making a prayer (rogación) on the head (Ebo Leri), a little of the compound should be placed on the nape of the neck to nourish this Eshu and promote it.

Being our biological Eshu, it is put into our body by Olofi as one of the components of Orì Inu since a few weeks before our arrival in the world. It enters our body through the cranial fontanelle (mollera) and remains sealed there until the time of our death.

Its purpose is to balance the life project presented by our soul before Olodumare before our birth.

This Eshu, along with Orì Inu, are the most important Orisha a person has on this plane, are the basis of their manifestation in this dimension and are the only Orì Inu that are born and die with the person.

He is an Orisha who does not have a necklace or distinctive colors to identify him. Since there is no agreement with him, it is said, "if your head does not sell you, there is no one to buy you."

It is recommended to perform a small ceremony on Monday that consists of refreshing it (the neck area) with coconut water. This ceremony will serve to repel low instincts, negative outbursts and explosions, as well as repel evil influences.

Orì Inu has the task of guiding the actions of the human being through the brain (called opolo). When an obstacle arises (some mischief of Elenini), it is the cerebellum (Ipakò) that performs the action through the body. Therefore, if we act correctly, it can be said that Orì Inu has overcome the obstacle of Eshu ni Ipakò.

In other words: when Orì Inu overcomes the obstacles of Eshu ni Ipakò, we can say that success can be achieved and the man raises his head.

Best Advice for New Olosha

1- Saints don't make mistakes.

Religion always leads you on the right path, but when some people do not hear what they want to hear, they feign religiosity and ignore the advice they have received. The saints and the dead will always guide you, but those who refuse to accept it are better off not seeking advice from the Eggun, Orisha or Orula, because in the end those who defy their word, disrespect these deities.

2- Everything you offer must come from the heart.

Offering pretty tureens and flashy altars in honour of our Orisha is different than speculating about them. True love is in the spirituality and mystery they contain. Let us remember that Orisha have always lived and dwelt in humble places, in tureens of clay and wood.

We must avoid between the habit of negatively criticizing others and bring out the "how you have it and how I have it". The strongest Oloshas magically are wisest have always had Orishas in very humble containers. In the eyes of the people their power was not seen. We must invoke, pray and chant our Orishas, try to unite our strength with that of our brother.

3- Ask with much faith.

Prayers to our Orisha if done with positivity, will and faith will take effect. Many people think that if you give a gift to the saint it becomes an exchange, this is not the case. The saints are there to help us, not to negotiate with them. They will provide whatever they decide is good or not good for you. Sometimes, without even asking, we offer them a party with drums; not knowing that Orisha only wanted a gourd full of fresh water and a candle.

Never tire of asking for health, peace and wisdom. Do not ask for money.

4- Learn from those who teach with respect and humility.

Approach true religious people who teach, guide and advise you with respect.

Don't let anyone belittle you, humiliate you, or feel superior to you.

5- Religion is carried in your heart.

I've learned, and it's been hard for me to understand, that everything comes when it's supposed to, even if you hurry. Our religion is not imposed on our children and family, we must teach them the ethics of our religion and precepts, but not force them to think and act the same way.

We give our hearts and show through time, with the patience of Baba Obatala that we were not wrong in giving advice and predicting what might happen.

Danay Donatien Martinez

The Royal Palm: Residence Of Three Fire Orishas

The most famous of the Orisha "Alafi, Rey de Oyò, Shangò", is inseparable from the most beautiful and striking tree in Cuba. Shangò (also called Olufina), as we have seen, lives in the Ceibas, but the Royal Palm is worth the honour of being the true home of "Alafi", his favorite and favorite abode, there he usually manifests himself in his most terrible aspect.

Shangò has other trees: the melodious poplar, the jobo, the framboyan, the cedar, the pine. The royal palm is the most symbolic of this deity who dresses as a fist, the beautiful and dark black one who eats fire, the "God of flames", the one who with the sharp and trembling rod of the palm tree that rises to the sky, shoots his arrows at the earth.

Where the Palm is, there is Shangò standing out on the branch, planted like the tower of his castle.

That bud that stands in the center of the graceful plume that his arms compose, is a true lightning rod that attracts electric discharges on itself. The lightning bolt, always goes to the Palm, falls into the Royal Palm. The association with the great Orisha becomes inevitable. Because of the lightning strikes a considerable number of these trees every year, especially in the rainy season.

The Palm also has an approximate value as sacred and important as the Ceiba in the religious economy of our people. The Ceiba is of the Most Holy, the Palma Real is of Santa Barbara, Shangò.

The Palma Real takes the lightning and keeps it inside. It has the power to bind the lightning. It is a legitimate tree of the fire family of Shangò Obakoso. It is the pedestal of Obakoso that devotees often come to confuse with Orisha himself, and claim "the Royal Palm is Obakoso himself".

Because of their kinship or affinity with Shangò, other Orisha participate in the cult that is rendered in the palms, among these Orisha we find "Oyà o Yanza", "Mama Oyà Ferekun", the owner of the spark, his inseparable and faithful concubine, who follows him everywhere and fights at his side in the fights. "Oyà Obinì dodo", is Shangò's right-hand man, the woman he loves and respects the most. When Shangò goes to war, Oyà is ahead, always fighting by his side with two swords, without Oyà's help, Shangò would have been defeated several times, like in his first war with Oggún. Oyà is from Tapa (Takua), from the same territory as Shangò. From Ilorin he went to Cuba, as this "soroyi" (song) recites: Oma do omo otaoma do amo otare bi iwa Oyà mala eleya".

Africans from Iyesà land say Oyà is "yesà", those from Takua say it is Takua, the Minapodos say it is Mina, but it is claimed to be from Takua (spelled Tapa). Often at folk altars the branch of a small brass palm tree supports a lead soldier representing Shangò. Toy palms should not be missing from altars as a traditional symbol of the "God of Fire and War".

Enjoying the Royal Palm, in addition to Shangò and Oyá, are the Orisha Aggayù "Strong Arm", "The Ball of the World", "Aggayù Solà", "Aggayù Larì". Aggayù (Babadina), owner of the land and the river, according to notes from African mythology was the father of Shangò, which is false since Shangò is the son of Obanlà. This mythological version, reinforced by highly respected African santeros, explains the following: Shangò did not know his father, who was Aggayù, he was so feared and respected that he left the door of his house wide open and no one would dare to enter, Aggayù always had his door full of fruits, since the river, the lands and the great savannahs were his. Shangò, however, entered his house, ate everything, stewed, and then lay down, in silence, on the same mat as Aggayù. When Aggayù returned from working in the fields, he found that bold boy resting, very relaxed.

- Hey, by golly! - said Aggayu. He grabbed him, gathered some wood, set it on fire and threw Shango on the stake; but Shangò did not burn. Then he carried him on his shoulders to the seashore to drown him, Yemayà (Yemayà Konla), Shangò's false mother, appeared in the sea and said, "What are you going to do Aggayù? You cannot kill our son." Aggayù then said: "In the world I am the bravest man and you Shangò are as brave as me, I certify that you are my son"; for this reason, the mythology continues, Shangò respects Aggayù so much.

Sometimes when he is angry or about to do one of his own, and whether in a holy festival or wherever he manifests himself (for given the temper of his nature he rages very easily and does not see what he is doing when he is angry), if Aggayù is present and intervenes, "Olufina" lowers his head. All that is needed is for the Orisha, as big as the pillars of the firmament, to stand beside him and look at him sternly.

"With one look the father rules the son."

"What belongs to the father belongs to the son," and although the Royal Palm is the acknowledged throne of Shangò, the rightful and universal heir of Obatala, it is also the property of Aggayù. The mountain is the staff of Olofi and the palm is the staff of Aggayù. The Ceiba is also the staff of Aggayù.

Aggayù and Shangò are two in one. By worshipping Shango, Aggayù is worshipped.

When a son of Shango is struck down, he begs Aggayù. Aggayù transfers to Shangò the right of residence in the Palm and the two together reign in the Palm. Both dress the same way, both are kings, they have the same temperamental, angry and warlike character, especially Aggayù. They are two orisha who cannot be separated and who eat together even if they do not eat the same thing.

Important details about Royal Palm

Several offerings are placed at the feet of the Royal Palm, and countless Ebbos are left in Shangò. They usually touch its trunk with 6 strokes, considering that it is the door of the house, then embrace it and with great faith and love invoke the three Orishas who reside there.

Palm leaves are part of the ritual costumes of Shango, also of the Oshosi and Oggun warriors. They wear a mariwò (a kind of skirt) over their clothes, made from the most tender leaves of the Palm tree that is to be placed on the waist of the Iyawó (the newly initiated into the religion).

The stems are also placed as curtains at the top of the entrance door of the Igbodun or room of secrets, where ceremonies and consecrations take place.

They are used on thrones simulating a mountain, according to the Orisha tutelary.

With the fibres of the Palm is made a brush used by Babalú Ayé that is called Já, it is also used by Naná Burukú. With the Já one makes ebbos.

With the wood of the Royal Palm, is made the Oché de Shangó (representative figure of Shangò), that goes inside its "Batea" and is a reinforcement of the king of the fire.

At the foot of the palms is where Shango throws his stones and after 7 years the sacred lightning stones come out of the earth (an attribute of Shango).

The santeros offer Shango at the foot of the palm tree, flour with okra, green bananas, fruit, cashew nuts and zapote or mamey (a tropical fruit that he likes very much). After receiving these offers, the palms respond and work.

The Royal Palm shakes especially in the Oni Shango (his children) a great attraction, it is something magical in his eyes, even without knowing that they are his children he tempts them to admire it. And it is that the royal palm is the irrefutable castle of the king of the drum.

It is also from this tree that we get the raw material to make the roofs of the houses and the hats to protect the lerí (head) from the sun.

So when you see a Royal Palm, greet it with great respect to the King of Fire: Kawò Kabiesile, Shangò Alufina.

Danay Donatien Martinez

The Dead And The Blood Pact

Why are the dead faster than the saints?

When you've been in this world of Santeria for some time you've surely noticed that the dead go faster than the Orisha themselves, and I'm not talking specifically about Eggun, the representation of our ancestors as life guides, but about something else , another gateway to understanding: the Mayombe Pole.

Why does the Nganga resolve faster?

The first thing that needs to be clear to understand the answer to this question is that when you work with dependent energies, you connect with their need. In the Palo, and even a bit in Spiritism, it is recurrent that the masters of this practice have a connection with entities of the other plane, let's call it: "dead", "spirits", "souls", etc. ...

It is for this reason that the Paleros go to cemeteries to look for bones in order to use them in a Nganga. But the Palero before taking those remains, must show respect and take the time to talk to that "entity" and reach an agreement or "pact". There they will establish the rules of the working relationship that will exist between the sorcerer and the dead man.

To clarify:

The dead/dead is an important link in this religion, it is an essential element.

A new initiate should not be given a Nganga (fundamento or take) right away. That would be like giving a loaded gun to a child.

That is why when negotiating this "pact" with the spirit, the scope and limits of this relationship must be made very clear to avoid misunderstandings and future disappointments. Especially since this "agreement" will be sealed with a blood oath. And this covenant must be honoured and respected by both parties as long as the person who intends to establish the partnership is alive.

But why do the dead work faster than the saints?

The reason is as follows; the dead will always do what is asked of them because they still maintain their consciousness and need to be fed. Its essence and strength is subordinated to the fact that they are reinforced/ fed periodically: either during rituals, with offerings. Also for the simple fact that being trapped in this plan without having a clear mission, many times they remain inoperative and accept the "pact" of the relationship that obliges them to obey. The problem with this situation is that the deceased, despite their condition, does not have the wisdom or worldview of the universe that the Orisha has, so the deceased just "comply" in exchange for what was agreed upon and many times without caring a bit about the consequences of their actions.

In the case of the Orisha, they have a higher spiritual level, which keeps them permanently in a state of virtue where they don't need the living or the dead. If you ask an Orisha for something and it doesn't meet their moral standards or fall within their scale of values, they will simply ignore your request. Their mission is to be guides and protectors. Not slaves to our whims.

That's why sometimes you have to know which door to knock on. Orisha will not always play in our favor, and less so if it is an ill-willed request. Unlike the dead, who are corruptible and sensitive to abandonment. You have to understand what is the difference between dead and dead. Not everyone is good, not everyone is bad. Some are brave and tough and some are meek and adaptable.

You must be very wise when you enter the world of the Mayombe Stake, for it is protection and witchcraft in its purest form. And many times in the wrong hands it would bring the opposite of what you are looking for.

El Palo is a spiritual elevator and at the same time it is a great responsibility, because what is asked with blood, is given with blood.

Ashè: mystery and vital force of the Orishas

What is this mysterious Asè or ashè spoken of in Santeria?

The meaning of the word ashè is the name given by the Yoruba people to the life force. Thus it is the invisible force and the sacred magical force of all deities, of all animate beings, of all things. It does not appear spontaneously, it needs to be transmitted. Any change in existing realization depends on ashè. And, in terms of force, it obeys certain laws:

It is reabsorbed able, workable, cumulative, and suffers the damage of wear and tear.

It is transmitted through certain material elements, certain substances.

Once transferred from these substances to beings or objects, the power of realization is maintained and renewed.

It can be applied to various purposes.

Its qualities vary according to the combinations of elements of which it is composed and that these in turn carry a certain charge, a particular energy that gives it a certain power of realization. The ashè of Orisha, for example, is nurtured through offerings and rituals, is transmitted by initiation and activated by individual behavior and rituals.

It may diminish or increase; but it never goes away. It remains present until the death of the priest.

Ashé is found in a wide variety of elements of the animal, plant and mineral kingdoms. It is found in the elements of fresh water and salt water, in the elements of the earth.

The animal kingdom contains ashè in the blood. And in this kingdom we include human beings, including menstrual flow.

The plant kingdom contains ashè in the leaves of plants, in flowers, in seeds (generators of life) and in honey, in a certain way an extract of the vital force of flowers.

As soon as ashè is present in human beings, it exerts its irradiation through:

- the breath
- semen
- saliva
- sweat and other secretions
- blood

In order to be able to act, the ashè must be transmitted through a particular combination that contains material and symbolic representations. This is the responsibility of the oracle and defined by him, the necessary composition of the ashè to be implanted and restored.

Animal blood together with the use of vegetables or minerals are the essential source for the restoration of strength. Every ritual, be it an offering, an initiatory process or a consecration, performs an implantation of strength and revitalization.

Ashe, the divine breath

Those who live, in order to be fulfilled or realized, need the use of ashè. And this is achieved through substitution, which is necessary and is achieved through ritual practice that has been performed since the time of creation.

The importance of regularity in rituals lies in the presence of supernatural entities and this is favoured by the activity of the ritual, practice being this privileged occasion for the transfer and redistribution of ashè.

The real religious difference is not the difference between those who worship and those who do not, but between those who love and those who do not. Between those who have genuine and true ashè, because not all those who claim to be priests and priestesses of Orisha and Ifá have ashè to transmit, because they were born to those who never had it, and therefore never received it.

This is one of the consequences of false initiations. This is why in a traditional religious family or lineage, the ashè that is transmitted from head to head is that which comes from the Lagba (elder) of said lineage, because he was the natural heir of the ashè of that lineage and, therefore, is the royal bearer of it.

The individual ashè is possible as a divine attribute of heaven, but this ashè is not transmissible to others as is believed, precisely because it is an individual ashè and not a collective one. Only the collective ashè, the one that radiates to the family or religious lineage, is the one that can be transmitted and empowered. It is for this reason that a priest or a priestess deprived of a religious family -or who for various reasons abandons his origin- loses the intensity and the strength of the ashè acquired by initiation within the religious family, because the adoptive families do not transmit ashè to these people. That is why it is advised never to leave one's religious family if one wants to maintain a living ashè.

Danay Donatien Martinez

How The Shangò Maraca Was Born

Each Orisha in the Afro-Cuban cultural tradition, has a useful magical tool to attract his attention. Some, like Oshun, have a bell. Others, like Shango, have a maraca all painted in red and white. The maraca has become a typical instrument of South American folk and popular music, also widespread today in pop music. Some maracas are made from an empty gourd, others from the fruit of a tree called "güira" in Cuba. But at least during the Shangò ceremonials they arouse both attention and a great energetic movement in the room of secrets also called Igbodu.

The origin of this magical instrument is told in the sign Odi tonti Obara (7-6) of the Diloggun, the divinatory shells that we use to predict the future and give solutions to problems. Indicating that the person must stop arguing with those people close to him, especially with his partner. This will only lead to divergence, and in the worst case will not come out of it because of a certain dependence sometimes insurmountable.

Just beware that a third person will profit from it.

Now let's cut to the chase and for you this little gem of Afro-Cuban literature that is still passed down orally in Santeria.

The Maraca Of Shangò

The story goes that the peony lived in harmony but one day the red part said to the black one:

-I am prettier than you.

The black part, in the same position, said to the red one:

-I am prettier than you.

And so they started a discussion about the beauty of each part. At that moment Shango passed by and when he saw those red and black colored seeds arguing so intensely, he said to himself, -If they argue like this, when I insert them in my maraca they will sound even louder."

And that is how Shangò's "maraca" was born, thanks to the discussion of the peony.

The Price Of Revenge In African-American Origin Magic

The orisha, the loa of the Haitian vodu and the Nganga, are entities that enter the life of the priest at the time of initiation or presentation to their cults. In the early days they manifest as restless energies, like 5 year old children, they know that they will have to wait for your requests and analyze your behavior in order to understand how to behave in your life. It's a programming phase, just like with computers. Then they grow up and become even stronger. The more time passes, the more they specialize in those issues that you choose to address with them in your magical and/or mystical career.

If you make your deities, work the dark side, they become "hot" and undisciplined. What's more, they leave out the good part of magic. They become very active and energetic, but they ask more often for animal sacrifices. And in the case of Vodu, they can also demand human sacrifices (not as seen in the movies, but in another way that I cannot explain here, but only in person). As time progresses you begin to become indispensable to them, they extend your life but feed on you. You are the one who becomes

97

their tool, and being undisciplined you have to submit to their will to keep them calm.

And when it comes to save someone, I mean to heal a disease, bring economic well-being, soothe a violent person, make mental problems disappear, you will have great difficulties with those gods you love to work with.

Fortunately, there is always a solution. Just tap into the help of those allies you "use" less. But you won't find yourself very loose in doing so, because everyone has their own way of working, a different cult. And getting to know them all takes years of internship.

I had evidence of negative, fast and deadly actions from a Haitian loa that came to me by pure chance, attached itself to me thanks to the years of working with my grandfather, revealed itself months after his death at a time when I was very sick. Today I regret directing him to the bad side, because I can no longer control him as I did in the early days, and when I call him he does his own thing. If I had put him on the good side, I would be protected by a life jacket, because it is a loa of the dead.

To describe to you how good it is to be good, I could give you the example of my grandmother, who has never worked magic. She has been crowned Oggun for more than three decades. Oggun doesn't make strange requests of her, and there is a relationship between them made up of prayers, dream dialogues, and offerings of fruit and rum.

When my grandmother was diagnosed with pancreatic cancer, Oggun made her stop chemo while she was doing her first cycle. The carcinoma disappeared. We're talking almost 11 years ago....

If Oggun had been set on the dark side of magic, he wouldn't have healed her. Maybe he would have, but he would have demanded who knows how many sacrifices.

In summary, a deity trained to do good will take care of making your life more pleasant, heal you and take revenge on your enemies without you saying anything. Or he will make sure to remove that person who brings you bad luck or suffering.

My advice is only advice. You are a person with the freedom to choose. I always tell my children: I encourage you and train you,

I try to bring you closer to the mystical side and I give you notions of magic, I also tell you how to kill with your orishas. After that you will do with them what you want.

For example, someone who is crowned Oshun receives in addition to Oshun almost ten orisha, if you want you can use one of those secondary orisha to work that hotter part. But you will have to be very good at working with that hot orisha.

Most of these teachings I received from an elderly woman who died three years ago, almost a hundred years old. And she made me think and understand better how the magical world of these African deities works. My grandfather had not touched the subject with me, but from that moment on, I understood why my grandfather specialized in getting criminals acquitted or released from prison and in making ligaments or love returns. He, even though he was Olo Obatala, had developed a very deep relationship with Oshun, with Oggun, with Shango, with Haitian loas, and three Nganga who are still at my grandmother's. When he died we found out that he had suffered a brain aneurysm ten years earlier, he didn't even realize it. Who knows what the hell wanted to keep him alive to keep doing those almost fantastic jobs?

But he was a machine, a living computer.

However, joining the priesthood doesn't mean starting a school where you'll get a degree as a wizard or sorcerer. Very often it is only the consolidation of a friendship, a fellowship with your deities. What you give, will be recognized.

Ofun And The Cult Of Ancestors

Ofun is said to speak not only of Orisha, but also of spirits of our ancestors, those who left a treasure trove of knowledge that make our lives more comfortable today. This knowledge includes not only scientific achievements and economic progress, but also those that tie us to nature and the domain of magic. I would say that Ofun recalls the more mystical part of the world of the ancestors, while Irosun speaks mostly of all that has passed and is now part of the earth (including our deceased loved ones).

If you remember the legend I told you about Ofun and the curious little girl, that little girl had discovered too quickly and without any regulation, a knowledge that turned out to be nefarious. Symbolically it was either a magic pot or a fetish, but what she saw was too much for her young age. So Ofun talks about a long journey of apprenticeship that culminates in the mastery and implementation of that cultural and traditional baggage.

Today I want to introduce you to even more about Ofun with a legend from the Diloggun literary corpus. Legends that have nothing to do with Ifa, because it's about Ofun, a simple Oddun. While in Ifa, all Oddun are composed following their binary system.

This legend has many keys to interpretation, but unfortunately they are reserved for the initiates, the priests who want to interpret the Oddun of the Diloggun and transmit to his assistants the advice of the Orisha.

Ofun and the cult of ancestors

Olofin was in his palace in the high heavens, it was a cold day or maybe he was cold, for sure he was bored. Nothing extraordinary was happening in Heaven and no news worth mentioning was coming from planet Earth. She decided to take a walk in the clouds that somehow seemed to be the same clouds of every day. Her best friend, the owl, was taking her daytime nap. She had been up all night and her daily nap was her only way to compensate for her perpetual insomnia.

So he found himself walking alone with no one to talk to. Feeling a little depressed, he parted in the center a bright white cloud moving directly over Oyò market. He looked down and saw Oya and Oshun who were Shango's wives at the time, and Yemaya, who was Oggun's wife, and had just arrived and joined the other two. There were a lot of human beings who, like the Orisha, were trying to get the best deals on all the things that the good Lord had put on this earth for them to enjoy. Everyone seemed to be having a good time. Everything was normal, maybe a little too normal.

Oya, Oshun and Yemaya were discussing whether or not to buy several pieces of vividly colored cloth, when this kind-faced old man came up to them pulling a rope to which a beautiful goat was tied and said to them.

"Ladies, I have a dilemma and I need your help. You look like three honest ladies. You see this goat, I need to sell it, but I have received a message from a dear friend and I need to visit him, so I don't have time to sell it here in the market. If you would be so kind as to sell it for twenty gold coins, I will take half of it and the other half you can divide among yourselves."

The Orisha women, being no different from mortal women, saw an opportunity to make some extra money without risking anything and immediately agreed to sell the old man's goat. It didn't take long for the beautiful goat to be sold and the three ladies, after separating the 10 gold coins for the old man, began to divide the remaining 10 coins. Yemaya counted them first, they were 3 coins each, but there was 1 coin left. She counted and counted, and each time it ended up being 1 coin left.

Then it was Oshun's turn to count them, with the same result.

A heated discussion ensued about who should get 4 coins instead of 3. Yemaya said. "It's only fair, the oldest among us should receive the largest share of this activity, so I'll take the remaining coin."

"No," Oshun interjected, "where I come from it is a ritual to allow the youngest person in a business to receive the best share. So the last coin belongs to me."

Then it was Oya's turn to speak. This question is up for debate. It is a well-known fact that when there is a disagreement between the oldest and youngest of the parties present, the reason for the disputed topic should go to the person in the middle of the two. As I am the one in the middle, I will take the last coin."

Needless to say, they couldn't get their act together. They looked for another Orisha who might be in the vicinity of the market square, but there was none. So they decided to call a wise man who lived near the market. When the man arrived, he took all the coins and made three stacks of three each. He finished with one more in his hands then said out loud.

"Well, I wish someone would tell me how I can divide 10 of anything into three equal parts? No matter what, you will always end up with one more. The question seems to be who is entitled to the last coin. I consulted with people who know about this sort of thing. They have told me that because she is the oldest of you to stay the longest in this world, she has suffered more than the others, which entitles her to better reformulations. It is my advice that we give the remaining coin to Yemaya."

Yemaya smiled smugly. Oshun and Oya's faces could not hide the disappointment and concluded that there was no way to accept her judgment.

So people started to get involved in the dispute. The market place became as crowded as a nest of fire ants with heated discussions going any way they saw fit to divide the coins. The sun was high in the sky becoming almost unbearable when they decided to call another person who would have to know a lot about numbers to help with this equation. The man arrived, took the coins in his hands, counted them and finished leaving one aside. He stood for a long time looking at it, after pondering for another period of time he said.

"There is no logical way to make an exact division of 10 between 3. That always leaves 1 excluded. The solution is to give the extra coin to one of the three people.... But to whom? I was taught that in a specific situation like this the youngest person should be the beneficiary of this equation and receive the remaining coin. The reason is that because he has had so little time on this world, he has received few of its benefits. The younger person is always rejected in play by his older siblings. The young hunter must walk behind the older hunters. The younger must expect to live a harder life. Therefore, when an even division is impossible, the youngest of these people should be justly rewarded with the extra coin."

He had just finished speaking when Yemaya and Oya, in not-so-friendly voices, said. "No one taught us such nonsense, so we do not accept your verdict."

And the crowd did exactly what they had done before. They sent for another man who was a wealthy merchant and knew about money deals. This man was a big, fat man with fingers full of jewels, who walked very slowly and had an incredible air of authority. The moment he arrived he looked at the coins, quickly separated them and continued to hold one in his left hand, then said.

"I see that the opinions are completely different. One group says that the last coin should go to the oldest person, and another group believes that the youngest person should be the beneficiary and receive the remaining coin. But the truth is that among you there is only one who is not the eldest, nor is she the youngest. Only Oya is older than Oshun and younger than Yemaya. Undoubtedly she is the one who meets the requirements to claim the right to the last coin. It is my solid advice to give the coin to Oya ".

Immediately this judgment was vehemently rejected by the other two Orisha. The situation began to get ugly with people taking sides as to who was entitled to the last coin. They were about to get into a fight when the kind old man who had given them the goat to sell appeared among them. The moment he appeared, a total silence descended upon the place. The old man said softly.

"Where is my share of the earnings in this little enterprise?" Oya went to him and gave him the 10 coins that belonged to him, saying. "Sir, you started this mess, could you please finish it?" The old man stood silently in the middle of the market as slowly his clothes and face began to change to look like who he really was and told him. "I am the father of you all."

And he gave three coins to Yemaya, three to Oya and three to Oshun. The tenth coin he held in his hand and leaning against the red ground surrounding Oyo, he began to dig a hole in it. When he thought it was deep enough he buried it, covering the hole until the ground was as before, then he stood up with all the majesty characteristic of Olofin and said.

"In the beginning of this world, not so long ago, these matters were settled in a simple way. Whenever someone, human or Orisha, received an unexpected gift, a pleasant surprise, or a blessing, they would separate a portion of it for the ancestral spirits. If it was a good harvest, a portion would be set aside for them, a good meal was shared with them. The offering to the ancestral spirits was a way of giving thanks for all the good things Olorun had bestowed on Earth. But you all seem to have forgotten this tradition. That's why I've come to remind you that tradition is what makes the family live in perfect harmony with the spirits of their ancestors".

Yemaya, Oshun and Oya as well as the humans in the village, both humans and Orisha agreed with Olofin and from that day on the tradition was kept by all Orisha's descendants and humans.

Ofun invites us to share the fruit of our efforts with Eggun.

Danay Donatien Martinez

Ofun And The Curious Little Girl

When I am interpreting Eleggua's word in the Diloggun there is usually an oracular sign that grabs my attention, as it warns of several things about the consultant:

He is unable to overcome a trauma or loss

He is under the effects of a curse

He is very attracted to the paranormal

His biggest flaw is curiosity

Someone is under strict surveillance

He is a very generous person, even too much so.

He has a very powerful mystical relationship with the spirit world.

When the Ofun sign came on the mat, my grandfather would leave the person sitting with the shells scattered on the mat while he went outside for a moment to make sure no one was chasing him. If possible, he would walk around the neighbourhood trying to see if any strange faces were approaching his house. Once he was sure there was no danger, he would continue his consultation with Eleggua. Ofun could even sense that a jealous woman was behind his godson's footsteps....

But Ofun doesn't stop with just these negative messages. There are others. We can think of several diseases related to the sign that depend on the main legend but also on many others such as arthritis, dementia, blindness by accident or progressive loss of vision and paranoia.

Ofun invites us to wash our eyes, because they are dusty. To keep our biggest secrets under lock and key, because someone wants to get hold of them.

But I think if you read Ofun's main Pataki carefully, you'll get a better sense of what I'm talking about.

Ofun and the curious little girl

Since Ofun didn't have any children, she liked to take care of other people's children. A neighbour couple and a friend of hers considered themselves "compadres", they had a little daughter named Anaganú, and Ofun asked them to give her to him to raise. The parents granted his wish and Ofun happily, installed the girl in his home, showering her with adulations.

Ofun was a deeply religious man who had penetrated many mysteries. He had a secret, a sacred object that he kept in a secluded place in his home, hidden behind a sheet of immaculate whiteness. Fearing that the girl, at some point when she was alone, would go to that corner with her toys, it seemed to her that she should warn her of the danger she was in if she discovered what was behind the sheet. Anaganú promised to obey and not to go near that mystery. But... curiosity is irrepressible, and at the first time, one day that Ofun went out to look for the girl's mother, who of course was visiting her daughter all the time, she pulled a ladder to the wall to find out what was behind that sheet. At the precise moment that Ofun and Anaganú's mother entered, there was a heart-breaking cry and the sound of something collapsing. Anaganú saw and what she saw frightened her so much that she lost consciousness and fell to the floor. Ofun rushed into the mysterious room and desolate picked up the girl from the floor.

"Give her back to me," cried the crazed mother.

"Fumi omomi ewa eni ko mi! Give her back to me as I gave her to you!

They put a curse on him! Oro jún ewani ko mio! "

Curiosity, all because of cursed curiosity.

Danay Donatien Martinez

The Three Bewitched Dolls

The bad investment of the three haunted dolls.

There was a man whose name was Lakin who lived in a small village. What made this story part of this Oddun is that in the same village lived a priest from Orumila who had a great reputation for miles around of being a great fortune teller.

The fact is that this man, Lakin, made a good business out of some goats he owned, but he spent half of his earnings having parties and gambling. When he realized what he had done, he decided to pay a visit to Orula's house to ask for advice on what to do with the rest of his money.

Orula told him to invest his money in things of value, to make some offerings to Eshu, and not to forget to give alms to the poor.

Lakin asked how much the offering would cost him. Orula told him it would be half of the money he had left. Lakin replied that it was armed robbery and that he would not pay a penny or make any offer to Eshu.

All the while, Eshu was in a room near where Lakin was standing and listening to what he had said. He took three dolls and inflated them with crazy spirits. In reality they were not really spirits, but some unknown creatures pretending to be human spirits. Well, whatever was put inside, the dolls looked and acted like they were real people, talking and laughing gracefully.

Eshu stopped on the road where Lakin was to pass and put the dolls up for sale. The moment Lakin saw them, he immediately liked them and asked what their price was. Eshu replied that they were priceless, as they were special dolls that acted as if they were really human beings; and furthermore, the man who owned them would become a rich and powerful man just by the mere fact of possessing such a unique privilege.

Lakin insisted and insisted that Eshu put a price on the dolls. Eshu practically made him beg for the sale of the toys, and eventually agreed to sell them for all the money Lakin had in his pocket.

When he got home, he put the dolls on top of the table and went to bed. There was no way he could fall asleep. The toys wouldn't stop talking and moving all over the table. He took them out of the house but the dolls kept talking and knocking on his door. Several days passed like that. Lakin didn't get a minute's rest. The damn dolls wouldn't stop making all kinds of noises. The toys were a nightmare!

Tired, with big bags under his eyes, he went back to Orula's house to ask what to do with the dolls. Orula told him that since he had not made the offer to Eshu, he had played a trick on him. Lakin promised that he would make a good offer if Eshu would take the dolls back and give him his money back.

Orula called Eshu, who was not long in coming. Lakin told him what he was willing to do in exchange for Eshu getting the dolls back and gave him his money. Eshu told him that only with a very good offer would he take the dolls back, but he would only give him half of the money he had paid.

Lakin had no choice but to accept, and it was the only way he could at least save some of his money and sleep at night. From that day on, Lakin thought twice before spending his money on silly things. He learned his lesson well, which is what this Oddun (7-6, Oddi tonti Obara) is telling you: be wise when spending your money and share your wealth with others.

The story/legend I just told is one of the many patakis that accompany the Oddun Oddi Bara or Oddi tonti Obara (7-6) of the Diloggun. Like all stories attached to oracular signs it inherently has a meaning that must be applied to the reading and would normally reflect the situation or moral conclusion needed. It is up to the person being read to apply the hidden message behind the story.

This is especially interesting because, although brief, it reflects the strange relationship between the Orisha and Eleggua / Eshu. In an abstract essence, they are counterparts: the soothsayer, reveals, clarifies the truths, the meanings of the natural order of things established by God / Oloddumare. In general, the soothsayer shows sympathy and may feel sorry for human weakness, which may be the reason why he is not just the "diviner", but more like the advisor on how best to behave. In other words: how best to avoid the unexpected, symbolized by Eleggua / Eshu, who is also fundamentally a disruptor / disturber of the order of things, and in his own unique way a teacher. A teacher who teaches us that we are subjects of the unexpected, of the unforeseen.

Defining the relationship between things, events, and actions, Orisha is the sensitive voice in a world of "cause and effect." While

Eshu personifies "chance," the accidents of life, the miscarriages of nature, all that is totally unpredictable. He is, in a form of free speech, genetic mutation. What Oloddumare intended to be in one way and came out the other way completely. I would call him "the great manipulator of life," and if one wants to have at least a modicum of control over what should happen and what should not happen, then by all means let Orisha tell us what to do to prevent or minimize Eshu's intervention in our affairs.

Danay Donatien Martinez

Why Is The Sea Salty?

A few days ago I did a consultation on behalf of an assistant. Eleggua showed the oracular sign Osà tonti Owani (9-11). An Oddun in which Orisha is telling the person to center his efforts in his own interest and future. The main proverb of this Oddun reads "keep walking, but look behind".

Osà is an Oddun of deep changes, of spiritual closeness to the Orisha and ancestors. But Owani speaks of vain efforts for the neighbour. So you can summarize this combination by saying that the consultant is very generous and candid in soul, but such goodness will not help him to progress.

And here I found this legend where Orisha notices the goodness of the devotee and gives him inexhaustible goodness. But beware, even those we least think of will row against our efforts.

The legend of why the sea is salty

Osaguere stood on the shore watching the endless waves of the sea. It seemed angry that day, rising and swelling with great waves that sent a cool oceanic haze over the beach. He watched the morning sun rise, looking not at the sun itself but at the path of the seething sun over the water, a path that ended at the horizon where the sky touched the sea. He disappeared into the cool ocean into an even bluer sky, into a gentle, sloping curve that slipped from view. She licked her lips, savouring the ocean mist on her skin. No water in the world tasted fresher than that of his mother, Yemaya. Gently he bent down to pick up a handful to drink before beginning his Ebbó.

Osaguere was a poor man, and the ebbò he offered that day was simple: on the sand he placed seven green apples, seven green pears, and bunches of green grapes; and then he stood back and sang the ancient songs of Yemayà as the waves reached out to the shore and sucked the offering into the sea.

"I am but a poor man, Yemayà," he whispered into the waves as the last of the fruit was sucked to the bottom of the sea, "and I need help. The soothsayers said you would help me if I made you Ebbó."

"I help everyone who comes to me with faith and ebbò," said a woman's voice.

Osaguere turned his head and froze; before him stood one of the most beautiful women his eyes had ever seen. She was tall, imposing, with pendulous breasts designed for nursing babies and tempting men, and a waist so small that it seemed at odds with her prosperous hips. Her face was dewy, rich and black, and her eyes like dark pools of ink Her hair was long and loose, coarse but held together by onions and shells woven into her locks. Osaguere's face was torn between astonishment and fear.

"Do not be afraid. You came here looking for me, but it was I who found you."

He threw himself onto the sand, rolling from side to side before resting his head on the ground. Yemayà bent down and gently touched his shoulders, blessing him; and then with almost supernatural strength helped him to his feet. They embraced orisha and human, and Osaguere felt Ashé like warm water flowing through his body. When they parted, he reached for her again; the feeling of separation was intense, like falling into a well. But Yemayà stepped aside and looked at him fondly. He felt naked under Yemayà's gaze.

"I live in more places than the sea, Osaguere. I watched you make ebbò. I am very happy. I listened to your singing. It brought joy to my heart. And now I have something for you. "

She accompanied him to a palm tree growing at the edge of the beach. Next to it was a mortar; but Osaguere noticed that it had strange markings up and down the sides. He stood next to Yemayà and even closer to the mortar, and something like a subdued humming sound seemed to fill his chest.

"All your life you have lived in the shadow of your brother, Osamoni. Everything is about to change."

Osamoni was Osaguere's older brother, and it was true: all his life he lived in his brother's shadow. Where Osamoni was brilliant, Osaguere was dull; Osamoni was handsome and Osaguere was simple. His brother was favoured by his parents while Osaguere was left to fend for himself in the world. And as an older brother, when their parents died he inherited everything, including the salt mines, and those mines were what made him rich beyond his wildest dreams. Osaguere remained poor.

"This is my gift to you, Osaguere." He looked at the stone mortar; it was slightly higher than his knees.

"I've seen some before, but normally they are made of wood. This one is made of stone."

"Yes, stone. Stone taken from the depths of the earth. Stone that lies deep beneath your brother's salt mines. I extracted the stone myself and with my own hands. My ocean flows beneath the earth in secret caverns that no mortal will ever see, and it flows beneath the ancestral salt mines. I took the stone from which this mortar was carved from that place, and carved it into a mortar with my own hands."

"Thank you, Yemaya." Osaguere looked at the mortar, puzzled, "But what am I to do with it?"

"Since the day your parents died, I have watched over you, Osaguere. Even though your brother inherited the kingdom, and even though he got the salt mines, you never became bitter. You did the best you could with what you had. And today you came to make ebbò. There was no bitterness in your heart. There was only love for me and hope for a brighter future."

"Anyway, what should I do with the mortar?"

Yemayá smiled, ignoring his question. "You didn't know that your older brother stole everything from you. Your parents wanted you to have half of their wealth. Your parents wanted you to have half of the salt mines. They wrote everything down on a piece of paper the directions on how everything was to be divided equally. But your brother found out there was this will and destroyed it. He who has your blood, the one who was once your best friend. As the oldest brother, he declared himself sole heir."

"He wouldn't!"

"He did. But this mortar makes all things right again. This mortar is full of Ashe and will make you a rich man."

Osaguere ran his hands over the mortar and felt something. He felt how the ashè flowed to the mortar from Yemayà, but it was not wet; it felt dry and warm and left a salty taste in his mouth.

"It tastes like salt," Osaguere said.

"Yes, this is the Ashé from the mortar. Just as your brother amassed a fortune from the salt mines he stole from you, so you will amass a fortune by selling salt. The mortar will give it to you." He approached Osaguere. "Pay close attention to what I teach you. Whenever you want salt, say these words: dance, mortar, dance and let the salt flow free! Now, repeat it so that I can hear you. "

Osaguere intoned the words and the mortar began to move, pounding the earth. Each time it crashed against the ground a pile of salt appeared. Quickly the salt spread around.

"And when you have enough salt," said Yemayá, "you say, 'Stop, mortar, stop, and let the salt be. " Now , repeat it so that I may hear you. "

He said the words and the mortar stopped. "That's great. I have to write those words down. "

"No!" said Yemayá. "The secret of the mortar is only for you. Never write the words down. One day you will be rich and your brother will be poor and you can buy back the salt mines from him. One day you will be so rich that the kingdom will be yours. And when that happens there will be no more need for the mortar. I will bring it back forever, far below the earth. "

Osaguere thanked Yemayà for all he had given him and with difficulty carried the heavy mortar home.

His wife waited somberly for him in the kitchen; she was cooking on a candle-lit stove. When he entered the kitchen, she barely looked up. "It's late. What did the soothsayers tell you?"

He kissed her lightly on the cheek. "They told me I had to make ebbò, and Yemayá would make me a rich man."

"The soothsayers always say that," she said. Her words were heavy, full of pain. She turned to look at him. "And did you? Did you do the ebbò? "' She saw the stone mortar he carried on his shoulders. She sat it on the floor with a great thud. She gasped.

"I did. And I saw Yemayá today. She came to me. She gave me this."

"Have you seen Yemaya?" His voice was thin and subtle. "In a dream? A vision? How did you see her?"

"She came to me and gave me this."

His wife smiled. Her husband was always a dreamer prone to telling stories about the Orisha. "And what is this?"

"A salt mortar. Look."

Osaguere softly sang the words Yemayà had taught him; his voice was soft and unsure at first, but as he remembered the words his voice grew stronger. The mortar shuddered and then jerked. His wife also jumped as he landed on the ground with a great crash and rose again. Underneath was a pile of salt.

Osaguere stopped singing. Over and over again the mortar rose and banged on the floor as if moved by invisible hands, and the pile of salt spread and grew. Soon the entire floor was covered with salt. His wife stood there with her mouth open and motionless, watching the salt grow around her feet.

"How?" -he asked her. "How do you make it stop?"

Osaguere sang again, only this time he spoke the words Yemayà had taught him to stop the mortar. The pile of salt beneath it stopped growing and spreading.

"We will be rich, my wife. We will sell our salt and be as rich as my brother."

She flew into his arms.

When Osamoni learned that his brother was also a salt seller, he didn't believe it at first. But when his palace guards verified that Osaguere was indeed selling salt in the market, he was disturbed.

"My brother sells salt? Where does he get it from?"

"We don't know," his guard replied. He and his wife sell it at the market and when they finish, they go home. A few hours later they return, with the cart overflowing with sacks of salt; and they sell it cheaply. "" But they have no mines. They have no workers. Where do they get it from? "

The guard remained silent.

"Find out!" He said. "Watch my brother in the market and when he runs out of salt, follow him. Look where he gets it. See who he gets it from. I want to know everything."

The guard did just that.

He returned later in the afternoon. Osamoni was waiting for him.

"What did you find?"

The guard was pale when he told him, "It's magic."

"It's what?" Osamoni's face was contorted in disbelief.

"It is magic. Your brother has a stone mortar that he talks with. He taps the earth and salt comes out of nowhere. He and his wife collect it after the mortar does."

"That's impossible."

"I know it seems impossible, but I watched him with my own eyes. He talked to the mortar while his wife was next to him, and then the mortar started moving up and down. It hit the floor hard before rising again. And each time it hit the floor, a pile of salt grew beneath it. After it stopped chanting, it continued to pound hard and the pile of salt continued to grow. I watched them bag it, more than they could keep up with! And then I ran over to tell you. "

Osamoni was silent. When he spoke his voice was thin. "My brother has always believed in magic and fairy tales. Even as a child he was devoted to the orisha Yemaya. He spent a lot of time with priests and soothsayers. Perhaps there is something to this after all? "He looked sternly at his guard." Do you remember these words he said? ""Yes. "He said the words Osaguere said to the mortar. Osamoni raised his hand.

"Stop. That's enough. I want you to get me that mortar tonight while my brother and his wife are asleep. Bring it to my ship. You and I will sail. We'll travel just far from land and I. I will test this mortar for myself. If it works, you can survive. "

"Yes, sir," the guard said before slipping away timidly.

"A magic stone mortar. Who ever heard of such a thing?" Osamoni wondered.

As Osaguere and his wife slept, the guard quietly entered through the front door. It was locked, but the guard knew how to pick locks and within minutes he was inside. His fellow guards were just outside keeping watch. He made his way to the kitchen where the mortar stood still; and with great effort he lifted the heavy stone over his shoulder. As calmly as he had entered he left; with his men he headed for the harbour.

Osamoni was waiting on the ship.

In the moonlight they set sail, following the stars just beyond the curve of the horizon where there was no hope of anyone seeing what they were about to do. Someone turned to look at the shore, its sandy beach glowing with the silvery sheen of the moon; they watched as it seemed to slip out of sight, swallowed by the ocean.

The stone mortar stood on the deck of the ship; it too shone in the moonlight, the hard white stone reflecting like a thick star.

"Do you remember the words?" he asked his guard.

He smiled and stood up. All the ship's crew came on deck to watch and listen. Softly at first, his voice unsure of the words he began to chant. The mortar twisted; it levitated slowly before crashing into the deck with a thud.

Underneath was a pile of salt.

"Keep singing!" ordered Osamoni.

The guard sang repeatedly. Again and again the mortar slammed into the bridge. Each time there was twice the amount of salt scattered on the deck; it grew and slid across the floor until the crew's feet were buried under it.

"Enough!" Osamoni ordered. "That's enough for now. Let us bag this salt and sail to the harbour. When we get closer we'll make more ... and we'll be rich!" The thought of effortlessly producing salt gave Osamoni visions of gold bars and others dancing in his head.

The guard stopped chanting; the mortar, however, did not stop beating.

"That's enough!" he said to the guard. "Make it stop."

"But I stopped," said the guard. Each time the mortar beat on the deck, twice the amount of salt appeared. It had reached the lower deck stairs and was spilling down.

"How did my brother make it stop? Do what he did!"

"I never saw him make it stop," the guard said.

"What?"

The ship began to sway under the weight of the salt. "We're sinking!" shouted one of the crew members. "Throw it overboard. Quick!" The guard reached for the mortar but as he grabbed it, he shrugged it off. Another crew member reached for the mortar, but he too fell. Still another tried to grab the mortar, but it fell on his hand, crushing him. The boat began to sink; and so far from shore that no one was able to swim back safely. They all drowned that day.

The next evening Osaguere stood on the shore looking out at the ocean. His mortar had disappeared, stolen with no witnesses to the crime, but Osaguere knew: his brother had been the thief. There was no other explanation. That morning, bodies had washed up on the shore, the bodies of his crewmen; and his ship had secretly sailed the night before. The men who stayed up late at the dock said they saw his guard carrying a strange object covered with sheets; they only knew it was heavy. They did not know what it was.

Osaguere had told no one about the mortar. And now that his brother was gone, everything his parents once had was his. Even without the mortar, he was a rich man. A light mist produced by the crashing waves and the endless ocean breeze sprayed his face; he licked his lips. The water was salty; it was no longer sweet.

Osaguere sighed.

Since that day, the sea has been salty.